SPACE

EDIT

RESET

AMERIKA YOUNG

Space Edit Reset

For permission requests, speaking inquiries, and bulk order purchase options, email info@thevividx.com.

ISBN: 979-8-234-01988-2

Published by The VividX House

Edited by Patricia Urban

Cover Art By Amerika Young

CONTENTS

INTRODUCTION

You want to feel proud of your home, but the rooms still don't feel right. You've spent money on furniture, and looked at Pinterest for hours. After a while, you may have stopped trying. You might even feel bad, like you should be able to figure this out on your own. After all, you're a full-grown adult, right?

You've already put in a lot of effort by cleaning, decluttering, and rearranging, hoping things would feel better. No matter what you do, rooms still don't feel good to be in, leaving you feeling confused and frustrated. No amount of moving sofas, rotating chairs or moving rugs brings lasting relief.

By this point, you've probably tried everything you can think of or you've given up because nothing worked. You've spent nights and weekends fixing the same rooms repeatedly. You've cleaned, organized, and gotten rid of things that didn't seem needed.

When you find a space on Instagram that looks amazing, you may wonder how to make your room look like that, too. You might not know why that room works or what to change in yours.

You've probably bought things online thinking, "Yes! This will finally make my room look better," but it didn't transform the room.

You hoped each new piece would fix everything. After all that, your room still doesn't feel right, and the frustration stays.

That cycle is expensive in more than one way. It costs you time that never produces lasting results, and you feel like no progress has actually been made. It costs money spent on furniture, storage bins, and décor that were supposed to fix something, but didn't. It costs precious space in your home, because your rooms go underused or avoided entirely. But there is another cost that lingers longer and cuts deeper, even if it's rarely named.

It costs you the confidence you have in *yourself*. You're great at many different things in life, but the place where you spend at least half of your time makes you feel stressed instead of relaxed. It leaves you feeling annoyed, tired, and uncomfortable, and you can't figure out what is causing it or what you should change to make it better.

You're great at managing responsibilities elsewhere in your life, at work or at school. You solve problems and make decisions. You handle complexity. Yet this one area keeps slowly eating away at you and the longer it goes unresolved, the harder it becomes to ignore that contradiction.

You respond to that discomfort in one of two ways.

You keep rearranging the room in every way you can, but the layouts get more awkward than the last.

Within days, the irritation returns and you're back to square one. The room still feels heavy and unresolved, so you move the furniture again. Ugh.

Or you might be the complete opposite type, avoiding the room entirely. You know it doesn't work, but you have absolutely no clue where to start so you shut the door and walk away.

Every room layout option feels risky, and you worry about making the wrong decision or wasting money. So, you manage to just live with it instead. You clean, wipe down surfaces, tidy counters and run the vacuum because you still like to be sanitary, but nothing in the room actually changes.

Whether you rearrange or avoid the space, you still end up disliking the room.

As you grow more frustrated, you head down a path that snowballs by swapping furniture that wasn't the problem in the first place. Then you buy all those fancy bins, baskets, and organizers because Pinterest told you to. The bins don't actually change the room. Last but not least, you consider remodeling or moving but that's expensive.

The Space Edit Reset will open your eyes to what's really going on in just one afternoon.

I bet you brought most of your furniture from your old house and put it where you could find a spot at the new house without thinking about what was really going to work in that space. That's normal. It takes time to see how you and your guests are going to actually use the room, and by then you just ignore how bad the setup is.

When all of this happens, the room begins to create problems immediately and these problems stack on top of each other. Then you feel like you're just bad at home design or décor.

As soon as I step into a room, I can tell within 30 seconds what the issues are and how to fix them. This wasn't something I was born with but a skill I learned, and by the end of this book, you will be able to see what I see whether that's in your own home or someone else's. Being able to see these things immediately isn't judgement, its awareness combined with systems for solutions.

When I enter a space, I briefly pause at the doorway and take in the room. From the doorway, the rooms almost always appear as if someone was fairly intentional in how they're put together and has done their best to tidy the space. To the normal eye, nothing stands out as obviously incorrect.

As soon as we step inside, I can see how the homeowner adjusts their body around the room without realizing it. This is where it becomes incredibly obvious to me how a layout and the items in a room affect your body and nervous system in that space.

I see things like a chair sitting close enough to the entry to narrow the main path. Everyone turns their shoulders slightly as they pass. A console table sits a few inches too far forward, compressing the walkway and slowing your movement as you pass it. Bags are shifted as one person pauses to let another through. These movements are automatic and learned through repetition. None of these moments is dramatic, but they add up.

I hear people say things to others in their house, such as "Ugh, why are you always in my way right here?" or "Why are we always in the same spot at the same time?"

How many times have you said this to your spouse or your kids?

You aren't annoyed with the other person running into you as you both pass; you're frustrated with the space and how it's allowing or restricting your movement.

People change their behavior to avoid the friction. They sit in the same spot every time because it's the easiest place to land. Guests hesitate before choosing a seat. People have shorter conversations because their bodies don't feel comfortable in that spot. The room is telling your nervous system, "This is a hard room to be in."

Every adjustment you make in the house is a response to the room's physical condition. Narrow paths produce hesitation or frustration. Unassigned surfaces produce constant reshuffling. The room creates the problem before you react to it.

Near the entry, a surface becomes the default drop zone for mail, keys, bags, and anything that doesn't have a clear home. The clutter isn't caused by laziness or lack of effort. It happens because the space was never set up to handle what actually arrives there every day. Even when the area is cleaned, the same items return because the underlying setup hasn't changed.

Just rearranging is not the solution.

Moving furniture around without understanding what your room requires changes the layout, but it doesn't change the conditions that created the problem; it simply moves it to a different location.

Doing nothing leads to the same predictable failure.

Stop and think about 2 things:

- What are the spaces or rooms in your home that have furniture, but don't get used often?
- What are the spaces in your home that become the catch-all for items that continually get piled up, no matter how many times you clear the space?

When you don't understand why a room doesn't work, every possible change feels equally uncertain and nerve-racking. Touching the space becomes stressful, so you manage around it instead. Cleaning gives you temporary or false relief. You tolerate the irritation with your space and assume this is normal or that you're just not good with design, but I'm here to tell you that you don't need a design degree to be good at setting up a home properly.

Whether you've been a serial re-arranger or frozen in your space, both have been a waste of your time and money. Both reinforce the feeling that this should be easier than it is.

This is usually the point where the issue stops feeling like a design problem and starts feeling personal. At first, the frustration feels practical. The room feels awkward to use, things are in the way, and nothing quite works the way it should. You assume you'll fix it later, once you have time or energy or a clearer idea of what to change. But when weeks turn into months, and sometimes years, the problem shifts. You're no longer just annoyed with the room; you start wondering why something seemingly so basic has stayed unresolved.

That unanswered question creates a quiet but persistent tension in your body and in the back of your mind. Each time you walk into this space and feel irritated, distracted, or stalled, it reinforces the sense that you should've been able to solve this by now.

Over time, you stop trusting your instincts in the room. You hesitate to make changes because past attempts didn't stick, and eventually you stop touching the space altogether because it feels easier to live with the annoyance than to risk another failed fix.

A room that works well feels easy to use. You don't have to think about where to walk or where things go. The furniture is in the right place, and everyday items naturally go back where they belong. The room fits how you live, so it supports your habits.

The setup should match your real life and daily routines. When it does, the room feels steady and stops draining your energy.

You were never taught how to check if a room actually works before trying to fix it. Most advice jumps straight to buying things, decorating, or moving furniture. That kind of help assumes the room already works.

When a room doesn't fit how you use it, those quick changes don't last. It may look better for a little while, but the same problems come back because the real setup was never fixed.

The Space Edit Reset™ exists because you were never handed a manual on *"How To Set Up Your Home Like an Adult 101"*.

Now you hold in your hands the keys to fixing this problem; a solution to your pain.

It's a six-step method designed to teach you how to evaluate what a room is doing, good or bad, before making any visual decisions.

Then you get to confidently decide what gets to stay or go, as well as where it should go.

Are you ready?

If you're more of a visual or auditory learner, check out the online course of the Space Edit Reset at

www.VividXHouse.com/space-edit-reset

SECTION I

1

The Modern Home Problem

Your home may have showroom-style furniture and tasteful pictures on the walls. Yet, despite having Pinterest-worthy stuff, something still feels off. This isn't a question of taste, style, or effort, but living or moving in this space takes a lot of effort.

Maybe your home is the opposite with a hodge-podge of hand-me-down furniture or items you've collected over the years.

Maybe you've told yourself, "Oh I don't care what my house looks like."

Maybe you do care what your house looks like, but have little clue where to even begin.

Have you ever been to a friend's home where every room is breathtaking, as if you could live there forever? Their belongings aren't fancier or more expensive than yours, but you can't figure out why their house is better? When you return home, you can't help but wonder why your house doesn't feel the same way. What's the problem?

The problem in your space doesn't hit you across the forehead and say, "here I am" or "this is what you're doing wrong." There are no broken walls or furniture in need of repair and no missing elements that would make everything click into place.

The problem arises from how you use your home over time. Some rooms don't get used much, and some you avoid. You keep clearing surfaces, but they fill right back up. You rearrange often just to make things work. Your house has all the furniture it needs, yet it still feels hard to live in.

From the outside, everything looks finished, yet inside daily life, the house needs constant fixing to stay usable. Cleaning and organizing help for a short time, but the same problems return because the setup doesn't support how you live.

After a while, you get used to the discomfort. The house looks fine, so it feels easier to ignore, but the frustration builds in small ways every day and slowly shapes how you move through your space.

You see this when rooms slowly stop being used as they were meant to be. Clear surfaces turn into drop zones. A room that once had a purpose becomes a place to store random things. It doesn't happen all at once. It happens little by little, until it feels normal and lasts for years.

When you first moved in, you probably thought briefly, "This is the bedroom, make sure all the sleeping and dressing stuff goes in here." Check. ✔

Then you put the rest where it "fits" and repeat the same process in each room.

From there, you joined one of two camps. You became either a "freeze in place" kind of person or a "serial re-arranger".

Frozen in place, you keep all the large furniture in the same spot and slightly shuffle the small stuff.

Rearrangers move everything big or small, looking for comfort.

Growing up, we had a big family room in our basement. The walls were brand-new, the paint was fresh, and the carpet was clean. It was the only room in the house with a TV, so we used it a lot. In high school, my brother and I moved our bedrooms down there because hanging out in the basement was the "cool" thing for teens. The family room was filled with a hodgepodge of furniture. We had antique pieces that my grandma passed down to my mom. A matching three-piece couch set straight out of the early 90's, some workout gear in the corner, and lots of other things we collected over the years. My mom and I rearranged the furniture a million different ways, but it never felt inviting, even though it was the family gathering place.

We struggled to define the different areas. We'd get the TV set up on a wall and the couch and chairs set up around it, but each end of the room felt like a grouping of random pieces that didn't belong together. The room spent more time trying to fit all the pieces than to accommodate how we actually lived. If rearranging furniture was an Olympic sport, my mom and I would have won the gold medal.

My nana was also a serial re-arranger, so I'm going to say we got it from her. Over the years, we added and removed furniture, decorations, and equipment, but the room still bugged us. Pinterest didn't exist back then, so I didn't have a place to look for "inspiration". Without the knowledge and experience I have now, I'd still be on that hamster wheel.

Eventually, we got the room to work for us, not against us. If I walked into that space today, knowing what I know now, I could help my mom put together a room that she loves in a matter of an afternoon.

How many hours have you spent scrolling Pinterest or following home-decor influencers on social media, wondering, "If I bought that new decor piece they're highlighting, would it make my home feel better?"

Influencers and Pinterest show you what to buy and what colors to decorate with. This only works if your room already has a clear purpose and can be used. When that assumption is wrong, decor doesn't solve the problem.

Think about your own space.

- Is it filled with random decor or furniture that doesn't really work together?

- Do you own nice furniture but avoid using certain rooms?
- Is there one room you never know how to set up or enjoy?

Your space isn't struggling because you don't care about it. It's struggling because it was never set up to truly work for how you live.

The Two Strategies That Keep Your House Unfinished

Are you a "serial re-arranger"?

When you're frustrated with a room in your home, a common response is to take some kind of action. Not because action is the right answer, but because living with unresolved spaces creates a deep itch inside to do something about it. You jump into motion, but you don't have clarity on what to do first. You think, well, something must need to move. A room feels irritating, so it needs attention. Before you know it, you're on a hamster wheel, making adjustments and moving furniture.

Furniture gets moved, rotated, swapped, or replaced. Layouts are rethought. Pieces are shifted by inches or completely rearranged. The room looks different, sometimes dramatically so, and that difference gives you a brief sense of relief. For a moment, it feels as though you've made progress. The house appears refreshed and your irritation is hushed. The peace doesn't last, because nothing about the room's role or setup has actually changed. The pressure simply relocates, and the house begins asking for attention again.

This kind of rearranging starts with small tweaks, then escalates into larger changes.

I mentioned my nana was a serial re-arranger. Every time we came to visit, something in her home had been rearranged. She had this old Victorian home, where the purpose of some of the rooms was up for interpretation due to an interesting layout. When she rearranged, you didn't know if you were going to be walking into a living room, a dining room or even a bedroom when you walked into the next room. I remember the large room at the back of the house sometimes being the living room where we'd watch TV, and sometimes it was their bedroom.

One time, my mom pointed to a picture hung in the most random space and asked, "Hey mom, why is this picture hanging here?"

Nana replied, "Oh, because there was already a nail there."

Talk about a palm-forehead smash moment, but can you relate to that?

My mom rearranged her bedroom and living room twice a year, with her "winter layout" and her "summer layout" based on where the heater vents were and making sure none of them were blocked by the couch during the winter.

When I was around 10 or 11, my mom opened my door and saw my giant sleigh bed with a tall headboard and footboard sitting in the middle of the room, and me behind a tall dresser. She asked, "What are you doing?"

I came out from behind the dresser I had slowly pushed out of the corner. "I'm rearranging."

"You are definitely your nana's grandchild." She said.

I wasn't insulted, I thought I was doing the grown-up thing and finding a better layout for my room. My bedroom (before I moved to the basement) was small, and the furniture was big, but I was determined to find a better way to lay it out. There was a lot of trial and error. I'd move the bed, wondering if it would look good in that spot, then I'd see that it looked terrible and not functional there. So, I'd push it or turn it to a new position.

This is how a new serial re-arranger was born. I'd keep rearranging all the way up until the day I got married.

Do you freeze in place?

This response looks calmer on the surface, but produces the same outcome. Instead of moving giant pieces of furniture around, do you leave the house exactly as it is? The room feels too unclear or overwhelming to approach, so you freeze, do nothing, and it stays frozen too. The furniture remains where it landed when you first moved in, and the layout stays unchanged. The house becomes something to manage rather than something to fix. Cleaning and tidying take the place of correction, and the setup itself is quietly preserved.

This approach can feel smart and careful. You avoid big messes and unfinished projects. The house looks neat enough, even if it's hard to use.

Over time, you get used to its limits, and then the room gets used less and less. The house stays standing, so it feels good enough, even though nothing really gets better.

Instead of getting a case of the "fix-it's," you get a case of the "forget-it's" and walk away from the room and attempt to block out the irritation.

What's important to understand is that these two approaches aren't opposites. They are variations of the same attempt to manage an unresolved setup. One relies on motion, and the other relies on containment. Neither addresses why the house behaves the way it does.

In many homes, these strategies alternate. A room is rearranged repeatedly until the effort becomes exhausting, then left alone for long stretches. The house moves between bursts of activity and periods of avoidance. During the active phase, there is hope that this time the change will stick. During the quiet phase, there is relief from not having to deal with it. Neither phase produces a lasting shift.

I've done a combination of both.

Three months after I got married, we moved to Florida to a 3rd-floor apartment with vaulted ceilings in the living room and dining room. It was probably built in the 80's or 90's, but had new cabinets and flooring throughout. The second bedroom was rather small, and needed to serve as both a guest bedroom and my office. We had frequent guests because people loved visiting Florida.

In this apartment, I was operating in both the serial rearranger mode and the freeze-in-place mode. My husband hated it when the furniture got rearranged in the living room or our bedroom, but he didn't care what happened in the guest bedroom because he was never in there. In our jointly used spaces, I placed all the big furniture and didn't move it, but in the spare room, I rearranged it as if it were my job.

I was working on writing my second book and wanted a dedicated place to work, so I was desperate to make something work.

I rearranged that little room so many different ways and hated every single layout. I'd stand at the doorway for what seemed like an eternity, and I'd just stare at all the corners of this room.

Why did I hate this room so bad?

Was it the furniture I had?

Was it the layout?

Was it that I was trying to cram two functions in one room?

I bought a new skinny desk, I painted a wall, I bought a new bedspread. I still absolutely loathed that room. So much so that I ended up avoiding that room and wrote most of my book while sitting in bed under the covers with a little lap-desk my husband bought me.

The office/guest bedroom became a catch-all space, and I avoided it until we moved. I went from constantly rearranging to full-on avoidance.

What keeps these strategies in place is that they feel like the only available options. Without a way to evaluate the house differently, rearranging and freezing are the two most obvious responses. One feels proactive, and the other feels contained, but neither produces a house that holds up to how you live.

Over time, the house behaves less like a stable environment and more like a series of ongoing experiments that never conclude. Until the setup changes, the problems will keep returning.

The Cost of a House That Never Gets Properly Set Up

A house that never fully settles, slowly takes more from you than you may realize. The cost doesn't show up all at once. It builds little by little over days, weeks, and years, and becomes part of daily routines. The house works, but not very well. It holds things, but it doesn't stay organized. It gives shelter, but it doesn't feel welcoming and easy to live in. Over time, the gap between a house that simply exists and a house that truly works becomes clear.

One of the biggest costs is time you spend fixing the same areas again, clearing surfaces and cleaning rooms. Each small task doesn't seem like much, but the time really stacks up. Constantly fixing a home that's working against you becomes a way of life.

I went through an organizing phase where I regularly threw things away, donated items, and "decluttered" anything I thought would help. No matter how much work I did, I kept looking at my space like something was still wrong. I'd fill up my trunk with half a dozen giveaway bags, drop them off at the local donation place, and unload them with pride, feeling like I'd done something to make a real difference in my home.

A couple of months later, I would get frustrated with the house and go on another decluttering and organizing spree. This process was on repeat. If I was doing the "right thing", why wasn't it making a difference in the long run!? I even did the "find what sparks joy" decluttering challenge. Yes, that made a difference in the things I got rid of or even how I arranged my closet, but internally I was seeking something with a greater impact on my home and my life.

The catalyst that opened my eyes to the depths of my frustration and time spent on my home was getting married. Here I was, the type of person who "loved" rearranging, and I married someone who hated it when things got rearranged. He wasn't against change necessarily, but the constant movement of things every few weeks wasn't his cup of tea.

Little did I know this would be the beginning of my mindset shift and of growing the skill of observing rooms, their functions, and properly *arranging* the room versus *rearranging* it from guesswork. I was no longer living by myself and getting to make all the design choices. I had someone else to think of; I was no longer solo, but had a new dynamic to take into consideration when setting up a home.

So how was I going to make a home work without the ability to rearrange it 1278 times before I got it right?

The Cost of Money

Money becomes another cost that slowly adds up. When a room feels annoying or hard to use, it often seems like buying something new will fix it. You may look for a new chair, a different table, better storage, or a piece that feels close to right but not quite there. Each time you buy something, you hope it'll finally make the room work.

When it doesn't fix the problem, the feeling passes quickly, and life moves on, but the cycle keeps going. More items come into the house to solve problems they weren't meant to fix. Over time, the home fills with things that cost money but don't bring lasting change. The spending grows little by little without ever truly solving the issues in the room.

Would you be blown away by the dollar amount if you added up the cost of all those decor or furniture items you bought that didn't work out as you had hoped?

Cost of Usable Space

Usable space becomes another cost. You don't have to have a 4,000 square foot home to live in a space that feels spacious, purposeful, and on-purpose. Rooms that are never properly set up rarely reach their full potential.

What's that corner of the room you avoid?

Do you have a formal living room that no one ever sits in, or a formal dining room that gets used twice a year, while other rooms in the house are heavily multitasking and used for multiple purposes?

That's the square footage of your home that you're paying for but not living in. Closets and corners are absorbing overflow because the house was never clear about where things should belong. The result is a home that feels both full and underutilized at the same time, a contradiction that becomes harder to explain the longer it persists.

As these costs accumulate, what could be fixed in just one afternoon, starts to feel like a giant overshadowing your life and home. Adjusting and rearranging no longer bring relief, so larger changes start to feel necessary. Furniture is replaced even when it isn't worn out. You've bought all the fancy storage bins, yet surfaces remain crowded. Renovations begin to feel like the only option. This leads you to feeling like you need a different home, a bigger home, or a better home.

What you don't realize is that moving to a bigger home, a nicer home, or a different home won't fix these problems. The same habits and layout issues often come with you. If you don't know how to look at the space you live in now and see what works and what doesn't, it's very hard to do that in the next home. It also makes it hard to know if a remodel will really solve anything.

A remodel may look new and fresh, but the same daily problems can return if the room still isn't set up to work well. The space may look better on the surface, yet the old issues keep coming back again and again. Changing how a room looks doesn't fix how it functions.

The modern home problem tends to last for years, because it works just well enough to tolerate and you delay making the right changes. That irritating feeling starts to feel normal.

The Mental Cost

There's also a mental cost to living in a house that never fully works, even when it's hard to explain. The house starts to feel unfinished. Each time you try to fix a room, and it doesn't get better, it can make you feel like the problem is too hard or somehow your fault. The home begins to feel like something you're constantly managing instead of something that feels settled.

It's important to know this isn't happening because you don't care about your space or because you're doing something wrong. It happens because most people were never taught how to set up a home so it works well. So, there's no reason to think you should already know this.

Pinterest and social media influencers teach how to decorate and fill your home, but don't specify whether these things will work for you or against you. Certainly, no one tells you, "Wait, before you put a single item of furniture or decor in that room, you need to evaluate it first."

Without that evaluation, rooms are expected to adapt indefinitely, and when they don't, the blame quietly shifts toward effort or taste rather than setup.

By the time this pattern becomes clear, the house has often absorbed years of trial and error. Objects have come and gone. Rooms have shifted purpose. Surfaces have been claimed and reclaimed. And still, the house remains unsettled. This isn't because the house is stubborn or flawed. It's because it was never given the chance to work for you, not against you, from the start.

2

The Body in the Room

Until now, you've experienced your rooms based on what you thought the decor was doing, but this book will show you how to pay more attention to the experience your nervous system is having in the room.

I'll use the terms "body" and "nervous system" interchangeably.

Long before you think about whether a room is helping you or making things harder, your nervous system has already done work to adjust to it. This happens without you noticing and without your brain stopping to explain it. Your body reacts right away by getting comfortable, feeling tense, staying alert, or pulling back. You don't walk into a room and think about how your body feels. You just start responding, and those reactions become part of your day.

Your body isn't paying attention to how pretty the room is or to its colors. It's paying attention to how much work the room will take to feel at ease in it.

Your body is asking questions like:

- How much effort will this space need to feel okay?
- How much fixing will I have to do before I can use it easily?
- How hard will it be to stay focused here?

When the room feels easy and welcoming, your body relaxes. When the room feels confusing or hard to use, your body stays on edge, even if nothing looks stressful.

What makes this hard to notice is that your body's first response to extra demand is to handle it well. Your nervous system is built to keep you comfortable and moving, so it makes many small adjustments without you realizing it. You still walk into the room and finish what you need to do, and go on with your day. Your body takes on the extra work, so your mind doesn't have to stop and think about it. This isn't a problem, it's your body doing what it's meant to do.

At first, these changes don't feel bad. They feel normal and even helpful. You may move a little faster, make quicker decisions, and do things more simply. Nothing feels wrong enough to fix, so you keep going. Your body is handling it for you.

Your nervous system starts learning patterns, like which rooms take more effort and which ones feel easy to use. It learns where starting a task feels smooth and where it feels harder. It learns where you can stay relaxed and where you keep needing to adjust. This learning happens through repeated experiences. What happens often starts to feel normal. What feels normal becomes your new baseline.

Have you ever heard the saying, "what fires together, wires together"? It means that your nervous system has sent a flare every time it has to adjust to something in your home. The first few times it might have felt slightly awkward, but then after that, the pattern became so familiar that your body now adjusts itself around the room without you even thinking twice. That awkwardness in the room just feels normal now.

As this baseline forms, your nervous system begins making decisions on your behalf without ever announcing it. You spend less time in certain spaces and spend less time engaging in others. You gravitate toward environments where your nervous system doesn't have to stay on guard. Your brain doesn't say, "Hey these choices are physiological responses."

You think these are just your habits or that you have a favorite chair or a favorite side of the bed. Beneath those explanations is a deeper truth: your body is conserving energy wherever it can.

When your body goes into saving-energy mode, it doesn't feel extreme. It feels smart and practical. It feels like using your time well and knowing your limits. Little by little, though, your comfort zone gets smaller without you noticing.

You stop doing things in your home that take extra setup. You put off activities that feel harder than they should. You pick the easiest option even when it isn't the most enjoyable. At first, this feels like adjusting to life, not like losing anything.

As this keeps happening, your body settles into a steady state where you're always a little ready for what's next. You aren't stressed or upset. You're able to handle things and get through your day. Still, your body stays slightly alert and prepared, as if something might need attention at any moment. Being ready becomes normal.

This constant readiness becomes part of everyday life. You may not notice it right away, but you feel it in how fast you move from task to task. You feel it in how rarely you fully relax in one place. You feel it in how finishing things matters more than enjoying the moment. You do what needs to be done and move on, not because you're rushing, but because staying longer doesn't feel very rewarding.

When your body keeps making these small adjustments for a long time, it starts saving energy in other parts of life too. You may feel less playful or spontaneous. You may become pickier about what you do. Rest may feel less, even when you have time to relax. You might feel tired and not know why, since nothing in your day seemed very hard. What's draining you is all the small adjustments adding up.

Because this change happens slowly, you usually don't question it. You start thinking this is just how life feels now. You may blame it on being busy, getting older, having more responsibility, or being in a tough season. You don't think about how the space you spend the most time in might be asking your body to work harder just to stay focused and comfortable.

As you keep adjusting, your body also changes how it sends signals. At first, signs of discomfort are easy to notice. Later, they become harder to feel clearly. When small problems aren't fixed early, your body doesn't shout louder. It switches into a mode where it just keeps going. It isn't giving up, it's being efficient. Your body stops asking for change and starts carrying the load so life can keep moving.

Endurance often looks like strength because you still show up and manage your responsibilities. You still function, and from the outside, nothing appears wrong. However, endurance isn't the same as support, and it's not the same as restoration. An enduring nervous system allocates resources carefully so it can keep going, rather than replenishing itself.

This is often the point where you turn the explanation inward. You assume you're restless, unfocused, or bad at relaxing. You tell yourself you should be more disciplined, more organized, more intentional. You try to manage yourself better instead of questioning why your nervous system never quite stands down. The environment remains unchanged, and your body continues compensating.

Your nervous system starts trading comfort for getting by. You stop expecting things to feel easy and stop thinking about what it'd feel like to fully relax in your own life. You begin to treat small efforts as normal and may even feel proud of how much you can handle. Still, getting by isn't the same as being supported, and this slowly changes what you think is possible for your home and for yourself.

As getting by becomes normal, you start ignoring your own feelings more often. When something feels wrong, you brush it off and tell yourself it's not a big deal. You may think you're overreacting or thinking too much about it. Your body learns that its signals aren't being listened to, so it sends them more quietly. The signals don't go away, they fade into the background, like a soft noise you stop noticing. If you pause for a moment, you might feel it.

Try closing your eyes, taking a deep breath, relaxing your shoulders, and paying attention to your body. Do you notice that low, irritating feeling you've been tuning out?

There isn't a big moment when everything breaks or a single problem that forces change, but your nervous system knows something is wrong

When you're home, it starts to feel like being wound tight.

Eventually, this shapes how you relate to yourself. Instead of the environment working for you, you hold yourself inside it because it's working against you. Instead of settling, you brace lightly and carry on. This doesn't happen because you chose it. It happens because adaptation filled the gap where support from your space should have existed.

None of this means your nervous system has failed you. In fact, the opposite is true. Your nervous system has been responding accurately the entire time. It's been doing exactly what it was designed to do in the presence of ongoing demand. You missed the signals because no one taught you to read this constant adaptation as information rather than personality or preference.

This is when a different kind of change is needed. It isn't about trying harder to stay calm or manage yourself better. It's about fixing the space that keeps making your nervous system work so hard. Your body can't fully relax in a room that keeps asking it to adjust. It can keep going and get through the day, but it can't truly rest while it's always working.

The next step doesn't start by trying to feel better in the same space. It starts by noticing how much work your body has already been doing every day in your home. It also means understanding that the answer was never pushing yourself more. The real answer is changing what your body has been carrying.

Your home effects everyone who lives in it, not just you. Think about your family.

- Have your kids been acting differently or having more trouble with behavior?
- Have you and your partner been arguing more than usual?
- Do you notice someone sighing when they walk into a certain room?

Those reactions often have less to do with their day and more to do with how their body feels in that space.

I'm in no way accusing anyone of being a bad housekeeper or being unorganized, but there are things in every home that silently eat away at every member of your household's nervous system, and everyone's symptoms of adapting are expressed slightly differently.

Capacity Loss and Normalization

When adjusting becomes your normal way of living, your nervous system doesn't just react in the moment. It slowly changes how it works to handle the extra effort. This isn't something you choose or even notice right away.

Over time, your body learns where it can relax and where it needs to stay tight. After a while, staying tight starts to feel like a smart way to live rather than a response to problems that never got fixed.

One of the first things to change is how much energy you have for life. This isn't about being strong or weak. It's about how much space you have to do things. You still get through your day and handle what needs to be done, but you have less energy leftover. You may feel less spontaneous, have less patience for small problems, and feel less excited about things that don't feel necessary. Life doesn't fall apart; you just start choosing carefully what you do because your body is trying to save energy.

As this keeps happening, your body gets better at using the least amount of effort possible. You spend less time on things. You avoid situations that feel hard or unpredictable. You choose easy paths more often. Being efficient becomes the goal, even when it means less fun or enjoyment. This change happens slowly, so it doesn't feel sudden or extreme, but over the years, life can start to feel smaller and more limited.

If this happened all at once, you'd feel like a frog being dropped into boiling water, and you'd jump out and say, "Wooo, wait a second!"

It's more like a frog being put into a pot of room-temperature water with the heat slowly being turned up. The frog doesn't realize the heat is getting worse; his nervous system just adapts until it reaches the boiling point.

Your space is slowly causing the heat on your nervous system to rise, and you don't notice it because it's one item at a time and not a truckload getting dumped into your living room. Your nervous system has learned to endure.

That's why it's easier to notice when you walk into someone else's home, and you automatically think, "Gee, how do these people live like this?"

You are not used to anything in their home, and everything that feels or looks off hits you like a ton of bricks or is waving a giant flag that says *fix me*. It doesn't have to be a dirty home; it could be a clean home, but you can instantly sense that things in this space are working against them, not for them.

Instead, when you go home, you slip right into it like an old slipper, and all you feel is familiarity. You don't have that "Gee, how do I live like this?" moment.

Your nervous system recalibrates its expectations based on what it has learned to endure. This recalibration isn't conscious; it's adaptive, and your body is constantly asking, "What do I need to do to get through the day?" and adjusting accordingly.

This normalization reshapes what you consider reasonable. You stop expecting your home to work for you rather than against you. You may even tell yourself that this is just what adulthood feels like, or what responsibility requires. The idea that things could feel easier stops occurring to you, not because it's impossible, but because it's unfamiliar.

How good have you become at tolerating what irritates you about your home or your space?

Here are some of the explanations you've given yourself:

- "I'm not good at organizing."
- "I'm not good at design."
- "My house is too old."
- "I'm not prideful, I don't care what my house looks like."
- "I'm too busy raising my kids."
- "I'm an entrepreneur, I don't have time to make a nice home."

- "Loving my space requires too much money."
- "I can't do this without a designer."
- "My house needs to be remodeled to actually work for me."
- "My husband doesn't really care what the house looks like."
- "I'm not trying to impress anyone."

Are you expressing a false humility by saying you don't really care what your house looks like, or you're not trying to impress anyone?

You don't need to impress anyone, but you do need to see what you've been tolerating. Before this, you haven't been taught to observe your home differently, or given the words to express what's wrong or what you've been tolerating.

I'm betting you've never heard anyone tie your nervous system and your home layout together in one concept. This isn't something you're taught growing up or taught in school. Your grandparents tolerated things in their homes that taught your parents what to tolerate, and most likely, many of those tolerated things were passed down to you.

Do you want to pass down that low hum of irritation to the next generation, or do you want to break that cycle for you and the people to come?

You've become really good at maintaining a sense of stability while under the strain of your space. You get better at pushing through. You get better at ignoring signals that don't seem urgent. You get better at functioning in a state that would have once felt unsustainable. This resilience is nothing to be proud of, nor ashamed of. It's something to call out so you don't have to be ruled by it any longer. This resilience and accommodation assume recovery isn't coming and reorganizes around that reality.

One of the more subtle effects of this is a shift in how you experience rest. You may have time to rest, but rest doesn't feel fully restorative. You sit down, but you don't quite settle. You stop, but something in you stays alert. Your nervous system doesn't stand down easily, because it has learned that standing down isn't safe or practical. There's always something to monitor, something to anticipate, something to manage.

Do you remember the long basement family room I previously told you about? After college, I moved home for a year and started my first "adult" job. My room was right off the family room, the one I had in high school. I grew up there; the space was familiar, but I had a new sense of unease I couldn't put my finger on. It seemed to roar much louder than a quiet hum. I brought home furniture from college and my mom helped me rearrange the family room once again, but I avoided it. Most of the time, I had the family room all to myself, but I'd walk out of my room, turn left, and walk up the stairs. The only time I really hung out in that room was if mom joined me to watch a movie, but when on my own, I couldn't bring myself to rest in that room. I always felt on high alert, like I couldn't rest because I needed to fix something.

I had so many happy, fun, family, and friend memories in that room, so it wasn't like something happened in it that I avoided it. I just didn't feel at peace.

At the time, I didn't have the vocabulary to express what was going on and why I tolerated or avoided that room. Looking back, I see that I had a much stronger and louder feeling of avoidance, because I had been away from it for a few years, and it was no longer cloaked in familiarity. I could sense it more clearly this time around. It was more like the frog tossed into the bowling water than the frog in the water that's slowly turned up.

Several years later, when I came back to visit my parents with my husband and stayed in the basement bedroom and family room, things felt different. Every time we'd visit, my husband would say hanging out down there was one of the most peaceful places he had ever hung out in. At that point in time, I could actually agree with him.

What changed from all those years growing up or coming home after college?

My mom was able to set up the room with two distinct zones that supported how she and my dad lived in the space. It supported how guests were supposed to use the space when they came over. Nothing was fighting for your attention, nothing was leaving you guessing, nothing was undefined.

Now it was one of the most inviting spaces in the home, the usual gathering place when everyone wanted to sink into a sofa and relax.

What's that one space in your home that you've avoided more and more over time?

Maybe you love being creative and using your space to make things. When your work area fills up with everyday clutter, it gets harder to create. Your energy for fun and ideas starts to shrink, and you feel less connected to it.

After a while, you feel like you're always managing and rushing to the next thing. Your home feels more about getting through the day than enjoying it.

You're not failing, but you're living smaller than you could. You still do life, but with less space, less energy, and less joy.

Everything you have been feeling in your home is absolutely reversible, but not just from internal effort alone. Your nervous system can't expand or relax while the same demands remain in place in your home.

Have you ever felt the joy and radiance in your body when lying on the beach, splashing in the ocean, and soaking up all the sunshine? Your nervous system is reacting well to the environment it's in.

Now compare that to walking down a bumpy dirt road where you have to watch your step, no leaves on the trees, it's entirely overcast, no sunshine, and a continual mist is falling, causing you not to be able to open your eyes all the way.

Think about your nervous system going back and forth between the two environments. You didn't change anything about your personality, your skills, or your habits, but your entire nervous system changed gears, changed feelings, and changed modes.

On the beach, in the sunshine, your body is entirely relaxed and at ease. You have time to think about that book you've been wanting to write or that project you've been wanting to start.

On the gloomy road, your body is tense, and you can't think about anything else but getting out of the cold mist and finding a dry, warm room.

This is an illustration of how much your environment affects your nervous system. You don't need a new home, but you do need your outer environment to change so your internal environment has a better chance at relaxing. When you're not compensating for your environment, your nervous system gets to stand down.

This is where the question shifts. Not "What's wrong with me?" but "What has my nervous system been accommodating for years in my home?"

Not "Why can't I relax?" but "What conditions make relaxation impractical?"

This shift is subtle, but it's critical. It shifts responsibility away from self-judgment and into clarity.

By the time you reach this point, you're often tired of trying to manage yourself. You've optimized, adjusted, and coped. What you haven't had is a way to remove the ongoing demand. Until that happens, capacity will remain limited, and normalization will continue.

This is the edge where a different kind of solution becomes necessary. Not another internal strategy. Not another way to tolerate. But an external correction that allows your nervous system to release what it's been carrying.

Not a decluttering session.

Not an organizing session.

Not a cleaning session.

Your Breaking Point

There comes a time when you'll reach your breaking point. It might not arrive as a dramatic moment, or it could feel like an internal explosion where you throw your hands in the air and say, "I give up, I need help!"

You may not be able to name what's wrong, but you can feel that the strategies you've relied on for years are no longer enough. Your nervous system has done everything it can to accommodate, and now the cost of that accommodation has become impossible to ignore.

You've reached your natural limit of endurance, and you're done compensating. You're done with that sense of friction that doesn't ever resolve. No more endless effort that doesn't make a real difference.

Maybe you're not in crisis, but you're not at ease. Maybe you aren't overwhelmed, but you aren't restored either. This feels unsustainable, even if it's difficult to explain why.

No more relying on internal strategies that fail. No more habits, routines, and coping mechanisms that once helped but no longer create relief. This isn't about being more disciplined, more organized, or more intentional, because that requires too much energy for too little of a payoff. Self-management won't solve a problem created by ongoing external demand.

At this point, something important becomes clear, even if only subconsciously: your body can't regulate itself out of conditions that require constant regulation. You can't meditate your way out of an environment that keeps asking for vigilance. You can't *mind-set* your way out of a space that requires continuous adaptation. You can't rest deeply in a place where your nervous system never fully stands down.

This realization probably brings you both relief and discomfort. Relief, because the problem finally stops feeling personal. Discomfort, because it means the solution can't be internal effort alone; something outside of you has to change.

Your nervous system responds to conditions, not your intentions. It doesn't care how much effort you put in or how much you want something to feel different. It responds to what's actually happening. When the conditions of your environment improve, the regulation of your nervous system follows naturally. When conditions remain unchanged, you continue to adapt, no matter how much internal work you do.

This is the turning point where responsibility shifts. Not as blame, but as placement. Up until now, your nervous system has been carrying a load that never belonged to it. It has been compensating for unresolved conditions quietly and consistently. At this stage, asking the nervous system to continue doing that work is no longer neutral, but actively limits restoration, capacity, and expansion.

What becomes necessary here isn't another strategy for managing yourself, but an intervention that removes the ongoing demand. You need something that allows your nervous system to release what it has been holding without first asking it to work harder. You need something that corrects the conditions in your home rather than asking your body to keep accommodating them.

This is where the Space Edit Reset enters the picture as a structural correction that finally allows your nervous system to stand down.

Your nervous system needs proof that it doesn't have to monitor, compensate, or brace.

This is why the Space Edit Reset doesn't begin by asking you to feel differently. It doesn't ask you to override your responses or manage them more skillfully. It works in the opposite direction. It changes the conditions of your space first, so the body no longer has to adapt in the same way. Regulation follows because the demand has been removed.

When your space truly supports you, your body starts to relax. You trust that your home works for you. Your energy slowly comes back because it's not being drained every day. You stay in rooms longer and use them more. It feels easier to start things and to rest. These changes are steady and real.

This shift has to be felt, not just understood. Once your nervous system feels the difference, it's hard to go back to the old way.

This is why, once the Space Edit Reset is understood and experienced, continuing to live inside a space that works against you will no longer feel normal. Your body will know the difference now. It recognizes when it's being asked to carry an unnecessary load, and it responds more quickly and clearly. Adaptation becomes visible instead of automatic, and you'll have the words to express what's wrong and a system to instantly correct it.

At this stage, your nervous system is no longer the problem. It's now your ally. If you pay attention, it provides accurate feedback about what supports life and what drains it. You stop arguing with your own responses, you stop explaining them away, and you begin using them as information.

This is the real shift that marks the end of the old cycle, because you became more aware, and have been handed the tools to change your environment. Your nervous system no longer has to choose between functioning and settling; it can do both.

The Space Edit Reset is about making sure your space works for you, not against you.

3

The Origin of the Space Edit Reset™

The Space Edit Reset™ didn't start as something I planned to create. It didn't begin as a system, a promise, or a product. Before it even had a name, I noticed what kept working, and it showed up repeatedly in many homes. No matter how different the houses looked, the same patterns kept appearing.

For years, people asked me what sounded like different questions, but they were really asking the same thing. They would stand at the entrance of a room, look around at furniture that seemed fine, and ask what they should do with the space. They talked about style, color, decor, and buying new furniture, but that wasn't the real problem. The truth is, they weren't confused about design; they truly wanted to know why the room felt annoying or hard to use and how to make it feel better.

Instead of giving quick answers, I began asking questions.

- How did they use the room each day?
- How did they wish they could use it?
- Which spots felt uncomfortable or got avoided?

While they talked, I watched how they moved and where they looked. I noticed which surfaces always collected stuff and which stayed clear with little effort. I paid attention to what the room seemed to pull people toward and what it pushed them away from.

I observed how someone might enter the space, move around, and where they might get stuck. I listened carefully to how people described the room and compared those words to what actually happened once the room was in use. There was almost always a disconnect between what purpose they wanted this room to serve and the way the room was actually being used or what it supported.

It was my personal internal system for helping clients without formalizing anything. I was simply repeating the same approach because it was the only way I could get to the root of things and have lasting results. I learned quickly that if I started with appearance, style, or color, the room might look better for a while, but it would eventually work against them.

If I started with buying, organizing, or styling, the room changed visually, but daily use stayed the same. The only time a room actually shifted in a meaningful way was when I looked at what it was doing before deciding what it should do.

I began noticing the same pattern repeating across homes that had nothing else in common. Different sizes, different budgets, different aesthetics, different people. Someone would describe a room as unfinished, frustrating, or wrong, yet nothing in the space was technically missing. Furniture, storage, and decor existed. What didn't exist was agreement between the room and the life happening inside it.

The instinctive response to that discomfort was always the same.

- Add something.
- Rearrange something.
- Organize something.
- Purchase something.

The assumption was that the room was lacking an element, and once that element was found, everything would fall into place.

I watched people follow that instinct repeatedly, with genuine hope each time. New furniture arrived. New containers filled the cabinets. New systems were installed inside closets. The room changed visually, sometimes dramatically, but the behavior inside it stayed exactly the same.

What became clear was that effort was not the problem; the issue was the order in which effort was applied. Styling and organizing were being used to answer questions they weren't designed to solve, and I used to be guilty of the same, until I learned. They were being layered on top of a room that had never been evaluated for purpose, movement, or use. The result was a surface-level change that didn't alter what actually happened in that space day after day.

Years ago, I helped multiple people with deep-dive decluttering sessions in different rooms. We'd fill the back of their SUVs with a dozen boxes filled with items from the room or cabinets and haul them over to a donation center. The clients were thrilled, and I would feel incredibly proud. I thought I was making a real impact on their lives. A few months later, I'd come by, and clutter had built up in the same places, objects had returned to places that didn't work. I had been treating a symptom, but hadn't yet created a system to address the root issues of a space, so all that hard work by both the client and me didn't stick, and the room was back to working against them.

This is when I learned that rooms needed more than just a decluttering session.

Later, I had a client who owned a dance studio and needed help with the office and storage areas. She was overcome by paperwork, a workspace that was almost nonexistent, merchandise that was impossible to access, and mountains of decor and costumes.

I had her walk me through every area of the studio and tell me what was working and what wasn't. I asked what irritated her the most. I listened to her words, but I also read between the lines. I was able to see beyond just what clutter needed to be sorted through. I didn't throw any design or layout answers at her until I completely understood how the space was working against her. This wasn't going to be just about matching storage bins or pretty labels. Don't get me wrong, matching bins and pretty labels will always have a special place in my heart, but they aren't the foundation of a space.

This dance studio was the first deep transformation I had brought to any space, where all the changes held up and worked for the client long term. We didn't just declutter; we reset the space in a way that worked for the client and not against her. We changed the office layout, so paperwork had clear, specific places to go, even if they were waiting to be filed or mail to be opened. All merchandise for sale was visible and accessible. Every change was made to suit how she actually moved through the space, in ways that felt natural rather than adapting because the space was taking over her.

When I look back, the steps were already in place. I had already been watching first and waiting to change anything until the room's patterns were clear. I removed things that got in the way before deciding what the room should be used for. I moved furniture after the main purpose was clear, and I added decor at the very end. The room wasn't finished until it could be used every day without needing to be fixed again.

When I worked in aviation as a private jet flight attendant, space was very limited, and mistakes had immediate consequences. Every item brought onto the plane had a clear job and a specific place to go. Nothing was set down randomly or left without a purpose. During takeoff and landing, anything not secured could become a dangerous projectile. There was no room for guessing or for items that took up space without being useful. I had to know where every single thing was before each flight began and ended.

Before every flight, I set up items in a certain order because there was so little space to work with. Even on the biggest jets, every shelf, counter, and storage area mattered. Walking paths were always kept clear. Moving through the cabin had to be easy and safe at all times. When a flight ended, the space was put back into its normal setup every time. The layout never changed. Doing this over and over trained me to notice anything out of place right away, because being out of place could cause real problems.

From working in that space, I learned that setting up and resetting go together. A space isn't truly ready until it can be returned to working order quickly and easily. I also learned that how a space works and how it looks are connected. A jet that works well but looks messy makes people not want to fly again. A jet that looks nice but doesn't work well creates stress and mistakes. Both are important, and one can't replace the other.

When passengers stepped onto the jet and felt good right away, it wasn't because the cabin was big or fancy. It was because everything had a clear purpose and was placed where it made sense. Nothing fought for attention or needed explanation. The space was already set up to allow people to relax and move easily.

Your home doesn't need to be expensive for this to happen. Any space can work well when purpose and setup come together.

As I worked on larger projects, the method became more important to me. I started writing down the steps I was already using so others could follow them without me being there. I wasn't trying to create something new. I was putting a clear system into words in order for it to work in any home, no matter the home size or value. Using the same steps in the same order kept bringing the same strong results. When people saw the process once, their questions changed. They stopped asking what to buy. They stopped feeling stuck in doorways.

The system removed all the guesswork by replacing it with a sequence of defined steps. The Space Edit Reset™ is not an organizing method. Organizing manages items. This system determines whether those items belong in the room at all.

It's not a styling philosophy, because styling just adjusts appearance.

This system corrects performance and purpose first, in order for styling and organizing to have something stable to sit on.

You wouldn't hang wall sconces on a new construction home before you pour the concrete foundation, build walls, and put up the roof.

You wouldn't put blush on your cheeks before you put on concealer, foundation, and powder.

These are parts of the styling, but not part of the foundation.

I created the Space Edit Reset™ because I tested every other approach, I rearranged, I organized, and I reduced volume. I even ignored rooms entirely. None of those approaches worked long-term until I realized that structure came first. Once it did, the outcome stopped resorting back into maintenance and adaptation.

I had the system long before I had the formal name for it. By giving it a name and writing out the instructions, I'm now able to share it with anyone in the world, even if I can't step into their home and personally walk them through it.

Why the Same Logic Worked Everywhere It's Used

What made the Space Edit Reset hard to ignore was that it didn't work just once or in a few homes. It worked everywhere I used it. It didn't matter what the house looked like, who lived there, or why they thought the room wasn't working. Homes had different problems, but the same steps kept fixing them. When people followed the process, the room came together the way it should have from the start. That steady result is what made the Space Edit Reset so powerful.

The steps aren't hard, but the order matters. By watching how a room is used first, you can clearly see what gets in the way. Your room shows what it can't support, and when you clear distractions before deciding what the room should be for, things become easier. When you let the room guide how furniture should be placed for that purpose, you'll stop guessing. Each time you follow the steps in order, the room stays working well. When you skip steps or change the order, you'll always have to fix the room again later.

I promise this works in every kind of home: big houses, small apartments, new buildings or in places over a hundred years old. Whether you have expensive furniture or pieces passed down, every outcome is a success.

When the steps are done out of order, the room stops working. When the steps are followed, the room naturally comes together and stays that way.

This is how you know the Space Edit Reset isn't about personal style or gut feelings. It's a clear system that can be taught and used again and again. It's a set of steps in a particular order that remove confusion and create spaces that stay easy to use every day.

As you use the Space Edit Reset as a step-by-step system, you'll notice a clear shift in how you interact with your rooms going forward. After doing the reset in one room, your questions and perspective shift as you start it in the next room.

Instead of asking what you should buy or where something might look best, you'll start asking what the room needs to support you in daily life. You'll stop feeling buried under the choices and options of what to do with the room. Fewer decisions are needed because the room itself makes the direction clear.

Your new sense of clarity won't be limited to one space, but it'll change how you look at your entire home. Once you experience what it feels like for a room to function correctly at a foundational level, you'll stop trying to fix other rooms by swapping decor or rearranging surfaces. You'll begin to notice patterns. The Space Edit Reset is no longer something happening to you; it becomes something you can recognize and repeat.

That recognition is important because it changes the story you tell yourself. Instead of blaming the room or assuming you lack design or organizing skills, you'll see the real issue.

The Space Edit Reset was first officially produced as a video course online and I had my mom go through it. I had no idea she was going to make my dad watch the videos and go through the steps with her. She told him, "If we are going to make changes to our space, you might as well do this along with me."

He happily obliged and sat down at the computer with her. The first room they selected was the dining room, but it was more like a combination of entry way, breakfast nook, and dining room all in one. This space was really bugging my mom, and things had to be moved when company came over. The number of furniture pieces in there was slowly growing, and the space was working against them. Through the process, they were able to see what elements had become catch-alls and weren't being used for their designated purposes anymore.

They could see which pieces of furniture didn't belong in there anymore and where others could be better positioned for clearer functions. They could see where traffic flow was being hindered. In a matter of one afternoon, they were able to clear their space, determine what belonged there, eliminate the breakfast nook, move a bench to the best spot, and learn how to use their dining table for eating only. They now have three distinct zones that work well.

My favorite thing was that after they were done, my dad insisted they do their bedroom next. He was unhappy that his dresser area had become a catch-all for all the little pieces in his life. He told my mom, "I want my dresser to look nice like my dad's dresser always did."

Before the Space Edit Reset, this was a thought in my dad's head, but he didn't have a system to show him how to achieve what he'd been hoping for with his dresser. It might not sound like a big deal to others, but it was a big deal to him, and that's what matters.

Through the Space Edit Reset, he was able to determine what was working against him in his own space in the room, and now he has the dresser-top space that inspires him and welcomes him. He was no longer guessing what belonged and what didn't.

My parents did the reset together in the bedroom, and now both have spaces designated for them that they love.

My mom and I talk about decor often, but it brought me immense joy to see my dad participate in the Space Edit Reset and how it transformed not only his space, but also his ability to see and observe it, allowing him to make the changes he desired. He even reset the garage!! Ha!

Seeing this result repeat across different homes, whether for family or clients, removed any doubt that the approach was situational. It works in large spaces and small ones, in shared rooms and private rooms, in places meant to be temporary and places meant to last.

The Space Edit Reset is about bringing a space to a state where it works consistently and without effort. It works whether I'm in your home personally walking you through all the steps, or you're reading the steps in this book, or you're watching the videos from the online course.

It's available at www.vividxhouse.com/space-edit-reset

When the Reset Entered Daily Life

When you experience the Space Edit Reset even once, your expectations change for good. You stop putting up with rooms that don't work because you now understand what a space feels like when it works for you and not against you. You can tell the difference right away, not because I explained it, but because the contrast is obvious to you. A room that works doesn't need constant adjusting, explaining, or second-guessing. When that becomes your new normal, going back to rooms that resist daily use no longer makes sense.

After you see the Space Edit Reset in action, you stop calling rooms "off" or confusing without knowing why. You can point to what's missing. You notice when a room was never clearly set up or when furniture was trying to cover a bigger problem.

You finally have simple words to understand your space, without feeling blamed or overwhelmed.

I want the Space Edit Reset to change lives all over the world, but real change has to start at home, because home is where the effects show up every single day. Long before the Space Edit Reset had a name, my husband watched me move through many phases of trying to fix our spaces, from decluttering to organizing to styling, each one helping in some way but never fully solving the problem.

I remember the first time I asked him to declutter his closet with me, and how strongly he pushed back until I asked him for just five minutes and I'd handle the rest. At first, he didn't see this as necessary, but over time, he'd gain appreciation for this.

Decluttering helped in the moment, but it wasn't the final answer, and neither was organizing or styling on its own. Decluttering primarily helped what was behind closed doors.

I have styled every apartment and house we have ever lived in, whether temporary or long-term, and those spaces often looked good, but the real shift didn't happen until the Space Edit Reset became a clear, intentional part of how we lived.

Once I began applying the steps of the Reset to our home and talking through the process out loud, my husband could see and feel the difference it made, not just in the rooms themselves, but in how we moved through our days.

He began to notice how different it felt to be in a space that had gone through the Space Edit Reset compared to one that had not.

Now, when something isn't working, he doesn't shut down or get frustrated without knowing why. He can name the problem and say that something needs to be reset, whether it's a surface, a room, or a space being used temporarily. Having that language has changed everything. It removes confusion and turns what could've become tension into something clear and fixable.

Instead of blaming each other or putting up with discomfort, the focus shifts to making a correction and restoring clarity, and the home returns to supporting us as we live in it.

Take a moment and think...

- How life-changing would it be for your family if spaces and things in your home no longer caused tension between you and your spouse or kids?
- What if they all had the vocabulary to share that the space needed to be reset instead of having their irritation come out as something else in disguise?

With the Space Edit Reset, you'll do the whole overhaul process for each room once, but in daily life, you'll apply the principles to do small edits in the room when life creeps in. It makes the maintenance of a room simple and easy.

As seasons change, family dynamics change, and room usage changes, you can repeat the full Space Edit Reset.

A nursery today will turn into a toddler bedroom, then a kid's bedroom and later a teenage bedroom. The Space Edit Reset is meant to help you grow with every stage and season of your life. Your home must keep up with your life and not keep you anchored to past stages. Once you learn the steps and skills, each life transitions in your home will become easier and less stressful.

Once you complete the Space Edit Reset, you may notice that it starts influencing decisions far beyond how you arrange your home. Without forcing it, you begin to slow down before bringing new items into a room and consider whether they serve a real purpose there. The Space Edit

Reset stops being a one-time process and becomes a practical way you evaluate changes, both in your home and in daily life.

What matters most is how this shift changes your relationship with problems inside your house. Before, discomfort often felt like something you had to adapt to or ignore, so you adjusted your habits rather than addressing the space itself. After the Space Edit Reset, your response will change. When something feels wrong, you'll no longer see it as a personal shortcoming or something to push through. You can clearly identify that the room needs correction, and you know how to respond without hesitation.

This change shows up in daily life in very practical ways. Rooms stop creating small irritations that follow you throughout the day. You aren't constantly stepping around things, moving items out of the way, or feeling distracted without knowing why. Small issues are handled early, while they are still simple, rather than building into frustration. Problems are addressed where they actually exist, so they get solved rather than managed.

You'll also notice this shift in how you make decisions. Once you experience a space that truly works, you'll stop questioning your own judgment. When something doesn't work, you can tell right away, and address it sooner rather than letting it linger. You don't become stricter or more controlling; you simply become more decisive.

The Space Edit Reset is more than a design system; it's a shared language for clarity. A way to identify when something needs attention without attaching judgment or emotion to it. It's a framework that allows you to intervene early instead of enduring that low hum of discomfort. That was never the original goal, but it became the most valuable outcome.

This is why the Space Edit Reset had to be documented. Not to package it, but to preserve it. Without a defined set of steps and shared language, the clarity it created would remain dependent on my presence. The goal isn't to make people reliant on me; it's to make the correction and transformation repeatable anywhere in the world.

Carry the Space Edit Reset with you, applying its logic wherever irritation appears, rather than waiting for things to become unbearable before acting. Then pass it along to someone else who could use it as well. You could help others transform their homes, too.

It's not something you grow out of. It doesn't belong to a phase of life or a particular home. It applies to a single surface or an entire house. It works in moments of transition and in periods of stability. The logic remains the same because the problem it addresses remains the same: spaces that were never fully set up are asking to be managed instead.

I don't care if you live in a yurt in Mongolia, a penthouse in Miami, a basement apartment in Denver, or an igloo in the Arctic. The Space Edit Reset works in every space and every phase in life.

SECTION II

The Six Steps

The Space Edit Reset will cause you to observe your home in a way you haven't experienced before.

You will notice:

- Flow vs. friction
- Calm vs. chaos
- Use vs. storage
- Belonging vs. buildup

The next steps aren't about instantly fixing what annoys you or making quick changes just to feel better now. Instead, the process deliberately slows things down so the room can reveal which parts help you, and which parts get in the way. Each step removes one kind of blockage, letting the next decision be made calmly and clearly. Rather than reacting impulsively, you're observing, then choosing what to do.

When the steps are followed in the right order, the room transforms naturally through how it's actually used, not by forcing anything. Nothing is forced into place too soon, and nothing is expected to work until the room is truly ready for it.

What sets this apart from your previous attempts isn't style or creativity; it's the order in which you act. You're no longer tackling a room by fixing whatever irritates you the most at that moment. That leads to a lot of activity, but the results are short-lived because the changes don't fit together.

With this approach:

1. **Nothing moves** until the whole room starts to make sense.
2. **Nothing is put back** until you know exactly where it belongs.

Because each step follows the one before it, the adjustments stick. The room eventually settles into a stable, reliable setup you can count on.

Getting Ready for the Space Edit Reset

There are four things you are going to need before you get started:

1. Your phone
2. 2 large baskets or bins
3. A large box with a lid or a closable top
4. 2 large trash bags

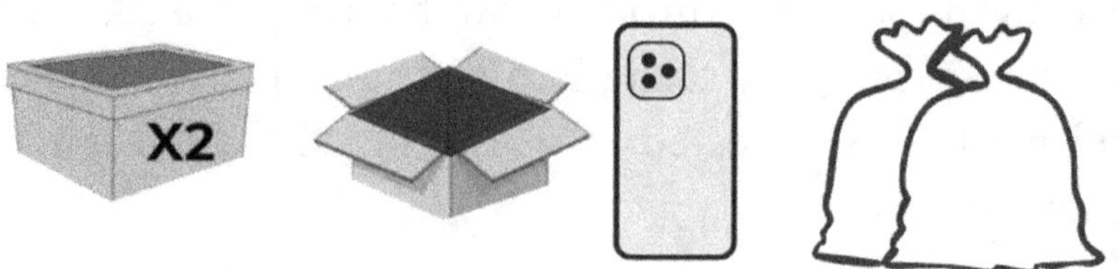

As you work through this process, make one promise to yourself: choose just ONE room to focus on and finish the entire Space Edit Reset in that room before moving to the next room.

Doing one room at a time will keep you from getting distracted and will help you keep the promise you make to yourself. We often break our own promises when we start something and never finish it. So, say to yourself, "I'm going to finish this one room before I move on to another."

During the process, the room may look very plain, even boring or rather empty. Don't let that scare you. I promise the process will come full circle. It can feel strange to see your space without all the items that have been crowding the surfaces and shelves for so long, but by the end, everything will make sense.

As you work through the steps, don't try to come up with ideas or try to fix the room right away. Your job is simply to pay close attention and follow each step in the exact order, even if you feel the urge to fix something or put an item somewhere "just for now." The order of the steps does the work for you. By sticking to it, you avoid reacting and making changes that don't last.

You can go through the Space Edit Reset by yourself, or you can invite your spouse, kids, or anyone else who lives with you. It's entirely up to you. Once you've gone through the steps, consider teaching the members of your household the process so they can help keep the home organized and working for you rather than against you.

As you go through these eye-opening moments, don't allow guilt or shame to take hold. The clutter and habits you uncover aren't a judgment of you; they're things you probably were never taught growing up.

When you finish all the steps of the Space Edit Reset, the room will look better, but that's not the main win. The real change shows up in how the room works for your everyday life. You can use the room without fixing it, adjusting it, or thinking about it. Things stay where they belong, and the room keeps working without you having to manage it.

ARE YOU READY?!

Before officially jumping into the first step, grab your phone. Yup, pick it up right now. It's time to take your 'before' photos.

Don't adjust or straighten up anything. The goal is to capture the room exactly as it's currently functioning.

1. Pick the one room you are going to work in for the whole Space Edit Reset.
2. Stand in the doorway or entryway of your room and take a picture.
3. Stand in each of the four corners of the room and take a picture.
4. Sit in your favorite spot and take a picture of the room from that perspective.

You should now have six photos. Save or store them. Don't delete them because you'll need them later for a before-and-after comparison.

STEP 1

Clear to See

Now you're ready to begin the first practical step of the Space Edit Reset - *Clear to See.*

Notice I didn't call it *'Clear to Clean'* or *'Clear to Decorate.'* Those are different. This step isn't about scrubbing, organizing, or styling. It's about creating enough space in order to truly see your room without distractions, layers, and noise.

This step is powerful because it sets the tone for what follows. Once you see clearly, you notice things you've walked past a thousand times. You begin to feel the room differently, because it now has the breathing room to show you what it's been trying to say. Let's step into it together.

Why You Begin with Surfaces

Surfaces are the landing pads of our daily lives. They catch everything. The things we put down for just a moment that stay for weeks. The mail, the mug, the keys, the book, the candle, the charger, and the pair of sunglasses. Surfaces hold the layers of our habits.

When surfaces are covered, your eyes never rest, which means your nervous system never rests. Even if it looks "fine," that subtle visual busyness adds weight. You might not realize it, but every object is a tiny pull on your attention, and when those pulls stack up, you stop feeling the room itself.

So, we begin here, not because these are the hardest areas, but because they are the most revealing. When you clear a surface, you don't just see a table; you see your habits. You see what you've been tolerating, and, most importantly, you see the room with fresh eyes.

Not Cleaning, Not Decorating

Here's what I want you to remember:
- You're not cleaning.
- You don't need to wipe or polish unless you want to.
- You're not decorating.
- You don't need to add flowers, trays, or books right now.

You're simply making it possible to see.

Think of it like clearing your mind in meditation. The point isn't to add in positive thoughts; the point is to quiet the noise so you can notice what's already there. It works the same for your room.

You're letting silence come before the music, stillness before the movement.

How to Clear

Grab your holding zone basket.

Choose your first surface.

Take everything off, one by one, remove each item and place it in your holding zone basket.

Don't evaluate yet. Don't ask yourself if you like it or if you need it. That comes later. For now, you're just removing every item from every surface

After you've cleared the first surface, move on to the rest and put everything into the holding zone basket.

By the time you've cleared all the surfaces, your entire room will look different. It won't be styled or finished, but the change will create space for awareness.

What Surfaces Should Be Cleared

Living Room
- Coffee tables
- End tables
- Shelves
- Chairs
- Console tables
- Entertainment centers
- Fireplace mantel
- Bookshelves (books can remain on bookshelves, but all trinkets, picture frames, etc. should be cleared off)

Dining Room
- Tables
- Serving cabinets
- Shelves

Bedroom
- Nightstands
- Shelves
- Bed
- Dressers
- Chairs

Office
  * Desk
  * Shelves
  * Cabinets

Kitchen
  * Counters
  * Island
  * Desk
  * Open shelves
  * Tables

If it's a flat surface, it gets cleared.

Now that surfaces are quiet, you may notice the artwork on the wall more, the scale of the furniture, or even the way light moves across the space. These details have always been there, but clutter masked them.

The Emotional Impact of Clearing

You may notice something surprising as you do this. Clearing a surface can be emotional. Sometimes you'll feel relief, almost as if your room just took a deep breath and the tension you didn't know you were carrying lifts. Sometimes you'll feel exposed, as if the empty surfaces make you vulnerable or uncomfortable. Sometimes you'll even feel restless, wanting to put things back in place to regain a sense of familiarity. These feelings might come up because our objects often anchor memories, routines, or comfort, and moving them can temporarily unsettle those attachments.

All of that is normal.

It's important to remember that you're not failing if you feel discomfort. In fact, that's a sign that the reset is working. You're not just clearing objects; you're clearing habits, patterns, and even emotions that have attached themselves to those surfaces.

This is why I want you to pause before decorating; that pause is where transformation happens.

Why This Matters

This step may feel simple, almost too simple, but it's the simplicity that makes it powerful.

When you *clear to see*, you're teaching yourself to pause before you act, to notice before you fix, and to evaluate before you add. This is how design becomes intentional rather than reactive. It's how your home begins to feel aligned with who you are now, instead of being stuck in layers of yesterday's habits.

The beauty is, once you've seen your surfaces clear, you can never quite go back to ignoring them. You'll start to notice when they fill again, and you'll crave that clarity. That's how this becomes not just a one-time reset, but a rhythm you can return to.

Closing Step One: Clear to See

You've cleared the surfaces. You've moved everything into a holding zone. You've stepped back and allowed yourself to see the room, not just the objects.

This may feel like a small beginning, but it's actually a significant shift. You've given your home space and yourself permission to listen.

As we move forward, build on this clarity. For now, live with the quiet and notice the difference, because transformation has already begun.

STEP 2

Sit With Your Space

Now that you've cleared your key surfaces and given your room the breathing space it's been asking for, it's time to do something that may feel incredibly simple, yet it's one of the most profound steps in the whole process.

I want you to sit in your space.
That's it.
No decorating, no rearranging, and no styling.
Just sit.

As you'll discover, sitting with awareness isn't the same as simply being in the room as you normally are. This is intentional. It's about slowing down enough to notice what your body and your nervous system have been trying to tell you all along.

Begin in Your Usual Spot

Start in the place where you most often sit in this room, such as your sofa, your favorite chair, or even the edge of your bed.

Sink into that familiar spot, the one where you watch TV, read, scroll on your phone, or chat with family.

Now pause. Don't distract yourself. Just look around.

What's the first thing your eyes land on? Is it a piece of furniture, a wall, a window, or perhaps a surface you just cleared?

- Notice what happens in your body as you take in the view from this seat.
- Do your shoulders relax?
- Does your jaw unclench?
- Do you feel a flicker of tension in your chest or stomach?

Your body is speaking. The cues may be subtle, but they're always there.

See the Room from More Than One Place

Move to a spot in the room you don't usually use. Sit in a chair you rarely choose, slide to the other end of the sofa, or sit in a corner if you're able.

Look around from this new position.

Notice what feels different. You may see how light hits a wall, an area you often pass, or a part of the room that feels crowded or open.

Pay attention to how your body feels here. Do you feel steady and relaxed, or slightly tense and distracted?

Now move to another unfamiliar spot in the room.

Look around again and notice what stands out this time.

Each new spot gives you different information about how the room feels and functions. Changing seats helps you see the space as a whole.

I suggest sitting or standing in 4 different positions or corners in the room to get a full 360-degree view.

The Nervous System Connection

Every room you walk into communicates with your nervous system through light, color, proportion, sound, symmetry, texture, and even the placement of objects. Your nervous system reads all of this before your conscious mind has time to think about it. That's why you sometimes feel instantly at ease in one space and unsettled in another, without being able to explain why.

When I ask you to notice where you feel calm and where you feel tension, I'm inviting you to tune into those signals.

Calm might feel like a deep breath; tension might feel like your shoulders tightening or your mind wanting to leave the space.

Neither is 'right' nor 'wrong.' Both are data. Both are your body telling you how the room is impacting you.

Reflection Questions

As you sit in each spot, ask yourself these simple questions:

- What am I noticing for the first time?
- Where does my body feel calm?
- Where does my body feel unsettled?
- If this room were speaking, what would it be saying to me right now?

Don't rush. Let the answers come slowly, even wordlessly. Sometimes the body speaks in feelings long before words.

The Story of the Room

Every room tells a story. Those stories could be:
- "I'm here to welcome you home."
- "I'm holding things that don't really belong here."
- "I'm waiting for you to notice me."

These observations highlight how objects and layouts interact with your emotions. Such insights can't be learned from a magazine spread or a Pinterest board. They come only from lived experience by sitting and being present.

Practical Tip: Stay a While

Don't just sit for a few seconds and move on. Stay for at least one minute in each spot. Let yourself settle.

Notice how the room feels once the initial novelty fades.

Sometimes the first impression is one thing, but what you feel after a few minutes tells the deeper truth.

Document the Experience

As you move through this process, jot down a few notes. Nothing complicated, just one or two words that capture what you feel in each spot.

For example:
- Sofa: cozy but busy.
- Chair: calm, open.
- Corner: forgotten, dim.

Closing Step 2: Sit With the Space

You've sat in your usual spot, then in unfamiliar ones. You've noticed what your body does, where it relaxes, where it tenses, where it feels most like home.

This isn't about fixing anything yet. It's about awareness. It's about honoring the signals your nervous system is giving you. It's about learning to hear the story your room is telling.

When you do this, you begin to see your home not just as a collection of furniture or décor, but as an environment that interacts with you, moment by moment.

From that awareness, the real transformation begins.

STEP 3

Emotional Mapping

Now that you've cleared your surfaces and observed your space from various vantage points, it's time for a step that may feel less visible, yet is equally transformative.

You're going to create your *Emotional Mapping*.

Up until now, you've focused on what you see and how your nervous system responds. Now you'll use words to name your experience. When you articulate what's happening in your space, you regain the power to shape it. This step isn't about fixing or deciding what stays. It's about noticing and putting your observations into words.

Think of it like journaling your home's autobiography. You're writing down what it's been holding, what it's been saying, and how it's been making you feel.

Why Naming Matters

Here's the thing: most people live in homes that feel "fine". Not bad, not broken, just... fine. And yet, when I talk to them, they confess that something feels off. They can't quite relax; they avoid certain rooms, or they feel inexplicably restless in spaces that should feel restful.

The reason is usually this: they haven't put words to what's happening. They sense it, but they can't name it. When we can't name it, it stays in the background, quietly draining us.

Naming what you feel in your space is like turning on a light. Suddenly, what was vague and unspoken becomes clear and tangible. Once it's clear, you can make conscious choices about it.

Focus only on clarity here. You're not fixing or decorating.

Guided Questions

You'll need a notebook or a notes app to write down your responses to a few questions. Take your time. Answer them from the heart, not from the head. There are no right or wrong answers.

- Does this room reflect how I live now, or a past version of me?
  - Maybe it's filled with furniture from a former stage of life.

- Maybe it's holding items you once needed, but no longer do.
- Or maybe it's perfectly current, but still carrying the energy of who you used to be.

- What feels supportive in this room?
  - Supportive means it makes your life easier, calmer, and lighter.
  - A chair that truly fits your body. A lamp that gives the right light. A rug that grounds the space.

- What feels like clutter, not because it's messy, but because it doesn't belong here?
  - This is key: clutter is not about quantity. It's about belonging.
  - A perfectly folded stack of papers can still feel like clutter if they belong in your office, not your bedroom.

- Which items feel like inspiration, and which feel like obligation?
  - Inspiration feels alive. You feel uplifted, proud, or comforted when you see it. Obligation feels heavy. You're keeping it because it was a gift, or it cost money, or you "should".

Write a few words or phrases for each. Don't analyze or try to fix - just name.

Digging Deeper

As you journal, go a little deeper. Ask yourself:

- When I walk into this room, do I feel energized or drained?
- Do I linger here, or do I pass through quickly?
- Does this room feel like who I'm becoming, or who I used to be?

Notice not just the physical weight, but also the emotional weight. Sometimes the heaviest items aren't the biggest ones. A single framed photo can carry a flood of memories that no longer feel aligned. A throw blanket can carry a reminder of obligation if it was a gift you never loved.

I want to emphasize that this isn't about guilt or self-blame, but simply noticing. Guilt has no place in this process, only awareness.

Short Word Prompts

If you get stuck, use simple words. Here are some examples:
- Calm
- Heavy
- Bright
- Restless
- Comforting
- Obligated
- Inspiring
- Distracting

Jot down whatever comes to mind. Even one word per zone can be powerful.

Once you've written down your words, go back and look at your before-and-after photos from Step One.

Compare your cleared surfaces to what they looked like before.

Can you tell the difference in the feelings of the before photos compared to your surfaces now?

Why This Step Matters

You might be wondering, why spend all this time naming feelings about a room? Shouldn't we just fix it?

Here's why: if you skip this step, you'll end up rearranging instead of transforming. You'll tidy, you'll shuffle, you'll style, but you'll never address the deeper misalignment.

When you recognize items that feel like obligation, you can choose with confidence. If a room reflects a past, you can shift it toward who you are now.

Clarity comes before change, and this step is how you get it.

Closing Step 3: Emotional Inventory

You've asked powerful questions:

- Does this room reflect who I am now?
- What feels supportive?
- What feels like clutter, not because it's messy, but because it doesn't belong here?
- What feels like inspiration, and what feels like obligation?

Whether you wrote a few words or many, you've captured something most people never stop to notice. Naming is transformative by itself.

Once you've put words to your space, you can never look at it the same way again. You'll begin to see it as a partner in your life, one that can either support you or hold you back. Now, you have the language to start shifting it toward support, inspiration, and alignment.

STEP 4

Evaluate What Belongs

You've cleared your surfaces. You've sat with your space. You've named how it feels. Right now, sitting just outside your awareness, is the basket of items you removed in Step One.

That holding zone basket is waiting for you, and in this step, you're going to resolve it.

What You Need

Items:

- Holding Zone Bin
- Shuttle Bin
- Box with lid (Later Box)
- 2 trash bags

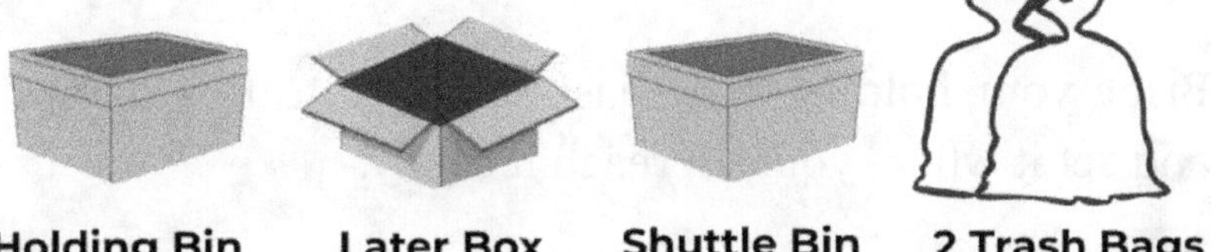

This is where awareness meets action, but in the gentlest way possible by asking the simplest, most clarifying questions:

- Does this item belong in this room?
- Or does it support me better somewhere else?
- Does it still belong in my life?

Why Belonging Matters

Each item in your home tells its own story. Some act as supporting characters; they belong in the scene, they enhance it, and they feel right. Other items are misplaced, like an actor wandering onto the wrong stage. When that happens, the story of the room feels confusing, cluttered, or incomplete.

This isn't about good or bad, keeping or tossing. It's about belonging.

When each object is in its rightful place, the entire room comes alive. The story unfolds, and the space finally supports you.

Begin With Your Holding Zone

Bring your holding zone basket back into this one room and set it where you can reach it easily.

You're going to empty it one item at a time, until nothing remains inside. By the end of this step, your holding zone will no longer be a source of indecision; it will be clear, resolved, and complete.

Pick up your first item. Hold it in your hands. Pause. Ask:

- Does this belong in this room?
- Does it support me better somewhere else?
- Does it still belong in my life or does it need to go?

That's it.

The Four Pathways

As you decide, every single item goes into one of four pathways:

1. **Belongs Here.** It supports the function and feeling of this room. It goes back into the room.
2. **Belongs Elsewhere.** It is right for your life, but wrong for this room. Put it in the Shuttle Bin and later it will be moved into the correct room.
3. **No Longer Belongs in Your Life:** Either trash or donate.
4. **Unsure.** You don't know yet. That's fine. It stays in a labeled container called the Later Box and is set aside for now.

There's no fifth option; no limbo. Each item gets clarity, even if that clarity is, "I don't know yet."

Belongs Here: Returning With Intention

When something belongs in this room, it doesn't just 'go back', it goes back with intention.

- Replace essentials: the lamp on the nightstand, and the book you're currently reading.
- Honor negative space. A clear surface is not empty; it's restful.
- Resist the urge to fill every surface just because it feels familiar. The goal isn't to repopulate; it's to align.

When you put something back, do it slowly. Notice how the room feels as soon as the item returns. Does it enhance the space, or does it clutter it? Let your body answer before your mind does.

Belongs Elsewhere: The Shuttle Bin

Some items may not belong in this room, but they still have a place in your life. Rather than wandering the house to deliver them elsewhere, which leads to distraction and overwhelm, grab an empty bin to use as your Shuttle Bin and place all the items inside.

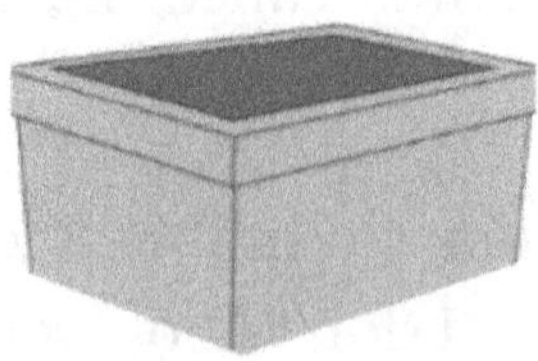

Shuttle Bin

The Shuttle Bin is placed at the doorway of your room. As you find items that belong elsewhere, place them in the Shuttle Bin and step back into your chosen room. Don't leave this room yet.

In the very last step of this process, you'll be instructed when to make a delivery run with your Shuttle Bin, but not just yet.

No Longer Belongs In Your Life

Even though this process isn't about decluttering, you will most likely find items that no longer belong in your life or are simply trash that you've yet to decide to throw out.

Place all items that are truly trash in a trash bag. Keep this bag open until you've gone through all the items in your basket.

All items that no longer belong in your life but are still usable should be placed in another large plastic bag and set aside for donation.

Unsure: The Later Box

Then there are the items that stump you. The ones that stir guilt, confusion, or hesitation. These are the things you're not ready to decide about.

These go into the Later Box.

The Later Box has three rules:

1. It must be lidded or able to be closed.
2. It must be labeled with today's date and the name of the room.
3. It must be stored out of sight, in a closet, and not on a surface.

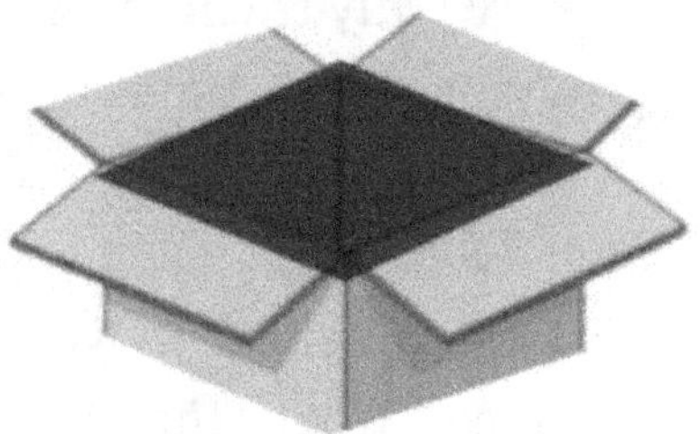

Later Box

Items in the later box often include:

- Gifts you don't use or don't like but feel guilty about discarding.
- Sentimental items you want to keep but currently have no place for them in your rooms.
- Items you truly don't know what to do with that don't belong in another room.

You don't have to decide today. You've already taken a powerful step by separating these items from this space. That separation creates clarity over time, and often, you'll find that after a few weeks, the decision becomes obvious.

The Later Box is not about avoidance; it's about wisdom. It honors the fact that alignment unfolds in layers. I'd rather see you place items in the Later Box rather than relocate them to another room, where they'll only contribute to further indecision and clutter.

Practical Examples

Let's make this real.

- You pick up a stack of mail from the dining table. Does it belong here? No, it belongs in the area where you handle paperwork, perhaps an office or command center. Into the Shuttle Bin it goes.
- You pick up a book from your nightstand. Do you actually read it in bed? If not, it belongs on a shelf or coffee table. Shuttle Bin.
- You pick up a candle from your living room. It feels right, and it supports the room. It belongs here, so place it back with intention.
- You pick up a gift you feel guilty about. You don't love it, but you don't want to toss it out. Feeling unsure? Into the Later Box.
- You pick up a piece of decor that doesn't fit your style anymore. Into the donate bag it goes.

See how simple it becomes?
Belongs here.
Belongs elsewhere.
Trash/donate.
Unsure.

Just four pathways.

What Completion Looks Like

By the time you finish this step, your holding zone will be empty.

- Surfaces in this one room will feel intentional and quiet.
- The Shuttle Bin will sit at the doorway, ready for its single delivery run.
- The Later Box will be labeled and stored out of sight.
- Trash will be disposed of, and donated items will be taken directly to the car.

No random basket of items left hanging. No half-decisions. Everything has been given clarity, even if the clarity is simply "not yet."

Notice the Shift

Stand in the doorway of this room and breathe.

Ask yourself:
- What eased when I placed things where they belong?
- What feels newly alive?
- What still tugs at me?

These are notes for your emotional inventory. Write down a few words, even just one phrase. This is how you track the emotional shift that comes with alignment.

The Delivery Run

Now, step into the final part of this process: the *Delivery Run*.

Shuttle Bin

Take your Shuttle Bin and make one lap through the house. Deliver items to where they belong. If you're not ready to fully put something away, place it neatly at the doorway of the room it belongs in. Avoid getting sidetracked with organizing or cleaning. Aim for alignment, not perfection.

Once the lap is finished, return immediately to your chosen room. You've just closed a loop that many people leave open, and that closure is a key part of what makes this step so effective.

The Difference Between Decluttering and Aligning

I want to pause here and remind you: this is not just decluttering. Decluttering says: "I have too much. I need to get rid of things." Yes, you'll have items that need to be thrown out or donated, but this isn't a witch hunt for "what must go?" When you trash or donate something, it's not about living with as little as possible; it's about deciding that something no longer belongs in your life.

Aligning says: "This belongs here. This belongs elsewhere. This one needs to go. And this one, I'm not sure about yet."

See the difference? One approach is about lack. The other is about alignment. This isn't about emptying your home. It's about allowing every item to support you in the right place.

Why This Step Matters

When you evaluate what belongs, you're not just sorting things; you're teaching yourself a rhythm of alignment.

You're telling yourself:

- I can pause.
- I can notice.
- I can place things with intention.

That rhythm builds trust in your home, your decisions, and yourself.

That's why this step matters so much. It's not really about the candle, the mail, or the book. It's about strengthening your ability to choose clarity over clutter and alignment over autopilot.

Closing Step 4: Evaluate What Belongs

You've taken every item from your holding zone and placed it into one of four pathways:
- It belongs here.
- It belongs elsewhere.
- It no longer belongs.
- You're unsure, and it goes into the Later Box.

You've returned what matters with intention. You've contained what doesn't belong in this room. You've given yourself grace for the things you're not ready to decide on.

And most importantly, you've emptied the holding zone completely. No more random basket. No more unresolved piles. Everything has clarity.

Now, as you look around this room, take note of how it feels. You're not finished; you're creating a space that truly supports you.

STEP 5

Subtle Shifts

You've cleared your surfaces. You've evaluated what belongs. You've released what doesn't support this room and placed the rest in your Shuttle Bin or Later Box.

Now you arrive at Step Five, which is where you might feel tempted to leap too far, too fast.

Don't be tempted to redesign your room, rearrange furniture, re-measure rugs, or re-plan layouts. That work is reserved for a full arranging session, which we'll cover in another section once the initial six steps of the Space Edit Reset are complete.

This step is about loosening what has been frozen, breaking the inertia of habit, and allowing the room to breathe in a new way.

Why Subtle Shifts Matter

Furniture and décor tend to get stuck. Once we place them, they rarely move again. Over time, we stop questioning whether they still serve us.

Spaces carry memory. When a sofa has been pinned to the wall for five years, the room starts to feel heavy, rigid, and predictable.

Subtle shifts transform the feel of a room without the overwhelm of a full rearrangement. Pulling a sofa a few inches forward can soften the entire space. Sliding a bed slightly away from the wall makes the bedroom feel lighter. Nudging a console table so it isn't flush against the wall changes the entryway from flat to inviting.

These micro-adjustments don't just change the room's appearance, but they also transform how your nervous system experiences it.

What This Step Is and What It Isn't

Let me be crystal clear: this is NOT rearranging.

Rearranging means experimenting by moving major pieces into completely new positions through guesswork. That's not the work of Step Five.

Here's why:

1. **It breaks the reset rhythm.** Rearranging throws you into problem-solving mode instead of awareness. This step is about releasing, not fixing.
2. **It creates overwhelm**. Rearranging opens a cascade of new decisions; where should the lamp go now, what about the rug, do I need a new side table? That's too much, too soon.
3. **It belongs in a deeper process**. Traffic flow, functional zones, scale, and proportion; those are the conversations we'll have during the full *arranging* process that we'll discuss later. That's where arranging is done with strategy, support, and vision.

In this step, I want you to resist the urge to rearrange. Focus on the subtle changes.

In Section 3 of this book, after the steps of the Space Edit Reset are complete, we'll discuss *arranging* with a plan rather than aimlessly *rearranging* without a plan. Arranging involves reconsidering circulation paths, re-balancing proportions, and addressing usable zones and traffic flow.

Here, in Step Five, your purpose is simply to loosen the room's position. To interrupt autopilot and open your eyes to new possibilities without falling down the rabbit hole of redesign.

Step-by-Step Subtle Shifts

1. Choose your anchor piece.
2. Pull it forward 2-4 inches. That's enough.
3. Step back. Notice the change in feeling.
4. Adjust the companion pieces.
5. All furniture items in the room should be slightly shifted to disrupt where they initially settled.
6. Stop. End here. Don't slide into full rearranging. Remember: restraint is part of the process.

Examples of Subtle Shifts:

- **Living Room:** Pull the sofa forward three inches. Angle armchairs slightly inward instead of parallel. Nudge the coffee table closer to the sofa.
- **Bedroom:** Pull the bed slightly away from the wall. Slide nightstands outward by an inch or two. Shift a bench forward at the foot of the bed.
- **Dining Room:** Center table under the light fixture instead of the wall. Angle chairs slightly to invite gathering.
- **Entryway:** Move the console away from the wall slightly so it greets you rather than clings to the surface.

What to Observe

After you make these small adjustments, pay attention:
- Does the room feel softer?
- Does your eye move differently across the room?
- Does the room feel more open, more alive?
- How does your body respond when you walk into the room?

These are the signals that tell you the subtle shift is working. These reflections keep you anchored in awareness rather than compulsion.

Closing Step 5: Subtle Shifts

You've broken the inertia of the room without diving into rearranging. By pulling pieces just enough, you've allowed the space to breathe.

You've loosened both the position and feeling, providing yourself a new perspective while resisting the urge to overhaul everything.

STEP 6

Reflection and Vision Casting

You've come to the final step of the Space Edit Reset.

Step Six is called Reflection and Vision Casting. This is where we pause to absorb what has shifted, and then begin to imagine what could be next.

What you've accomplished in the previous steps goes beyond mere clearing, evaluating, or shifting furniture. You've reset how you see your home. Once you see your space with clarity, it's a viewpoint you can't unsee. That clarity becomes the seed for your home's transformation.

Capture the Shift

Before we proceed, I want you to repeat the photos you began with. Pick up your phone and take photos from the exact same six perspectives you used in Step One:

- All four corners of the room.
- Your favorite spot in the room.
- The entry of the room.

Take your time. Stand in the same place, and frame the same views.

Swipe between your before and after photos, and notice what has changed. Notice what feels lighter. Notice how much clarity you've created, even without decorating, rearranging, or adding anything new.

This is proof that even the simplest reset can create real, visible, and felt change.

Why Reflection Matters

Don't skip or rush through reflection or move on too quickly, in search of the next project or fix. Reflection is what seals the shift you've made.

This reset isn't just about your room, it's about you. Every decision you've made here is also a declaration:

- I am capable of clarity.

- I can create alignment.
- I can keep a promise to myself.
- I am willing to live with intention instead of autopilot.

Take a moment to pause and let yourself feel that. You've already proven you can transform your home, not by spending money or purchasing new items, but by observing, shifting, and aligning.

Vision Casting: Looking Ahead

Now, let's turn toward the future.

Your room is quieter, clearer, and looser. You've created space, but remember, it's not the end; it's the beginning.

Close your eyes for a moment. Imagine walking into this room six months from now. Imagine it fully aligned with the life you're stepping into.

- What word rises up to describe it? Calm? Energized? Inviting? Luxurious?
- How do you feel when you walk through the door?
- What happens in your body? Do you breathe deeper? Do you stand taller?
- When others enter this space, what do you want them to feel?

There are no wrong answers. The words that come to you serve as your compass. They represent the language of your vision.

Closing Step 6: Reflection & Vision Casting

You've seen the room before and after. You've felt how the space changes when it's clear, purposeful, and easy to use. You now understand what makes a room work.

This is the moment everything clicks.

You're no longer guessing why a space feels off or trying random fixes to improve it. Instead, you can clearly identify what supports the room, what gets in the way, and how small shifts can transform how the space functions.

You did it.

You've learned how to reset a room so it works for you instead of against you.

This isn't a one-time solution. It's a skill you carry into every season of life. As routines change, families grow, work shifts, and needs evolve, you now possess the ability to restore clarity and ease in any room.

From this point forward, your home doesn't have to drift into frustration again. You know how to recognize when a space stops working and how to reset it with confidence.

This is how your rooms remain steady, supportive, and easy to live in, regardless of what life brings.

The next section covers arranging your rooms properly. Arranging will change the structure of a room, and it will be able to continue working for you in that position for years. When your room is properly arranged, it's possible for the loose items in your room to start working against you over time. The Space Edit Reset will be easier in the future, because you won't be fighting the layout of the large furniture, but resetting the smaller or loose items.

Share your before and after photos online!

Use #SpaceEditReset.

Tag: @TheVividXHouse

Facebook Group: Space Edit Reset

Instagram @TheVividXHouse

TikTok: @TheVividXHouse

Are you a visual or auditory learner?

You already know the Space Edit Reset works.

If you want to move faster and cut the guesswork, the online course shows the reset step by step.

No trial and error. No second-guessing.

You can pause, replay, and reset your own room the same day.

The book gives you the system.
The videos give you execution.

If you want cleaner results with fewer mistakes, the walkthroughs turn every reset into a clear, repeatable process.

Visit www.vividxhouse.com/space-edit-reset

SECTION III

Arranging VS Rearranging

I separated the Space Edit Reset from the arranging process because arranging can change the structural integrity of a room. Before you can properly arrange a space, it's essential to determine what belongs and what doesn't. I'm proud of you for completing the Space Edit Reset.

Previously, you may have felt you were bad at arranging, but it was really just a matter of timing. Now that the reset is complete, you're ready to embrace the process.

No more being a serial re-arranger like I was growing up. You finally have the freedom to arrange with intention and purpose.

It'll transform your experience from simply existing in your room to walking in with the confidence of someone who hired a designer. You'll possess the skills to create a space that truly works for you. When a guest falls in love with your home, you can proudly share that you did it all yourself.

I have provided instructions and diagrams to help you set up and arrange each area of your home. The emphasis will be on creating symmetry in each room, as your eyes and nervous system naturally feel more at ease when things are symmetrical. You'll be able to arrange furniture in a way that not only looks fantastic, but also makes you feel great spending time there.

Arranging the Bedroom

Arranging a bedroom starts with one main choice: the placement of the bed. Once the Space Edit Reset™ is complete, the room should be free of unnecessary items. Anything that doesn't contribute to sleeping, getting ready, or moving through the space should be removed.

The goal now is to create symmetry and ensure easy access to and from the bed. Since the bed is the largest piece in the room, everything else should be arranged around it.

When the bed is positioned poorly, the room feels unbalanced, leading you to constantly rearrange other items. When the bed is in an optimal spot, placing the rest of the furniture becomes easier, and it tends to stay in place.

Step One: Choose the Wall That Can Support the Bed

Begin by looking around the room to identify the wall that works best for the bed. Typically, this will be the largest, clearest, and most open wall.

Avoid choosing a wall simply because the bed has always been there or because it feels convenient. Center the bed on this wall.

Step Two: Center the Bed to Establish Balance

Choose the wall and place the bed in the middle of it. This makes the room easier to walk through and easier to use.

When the bed is centered, you can walk on both sides without squeezing or favoring one side. Both sides feel open and easy to reach. After you place the bed, walk around it and notice how it feels. If one side feels tight, slide the bed over until both sides feel comfortable.

The bed doesn't need to be pressed against the wall. Leaving a small space behind the headboard is fine as long as the bed feels steady and stays in place.

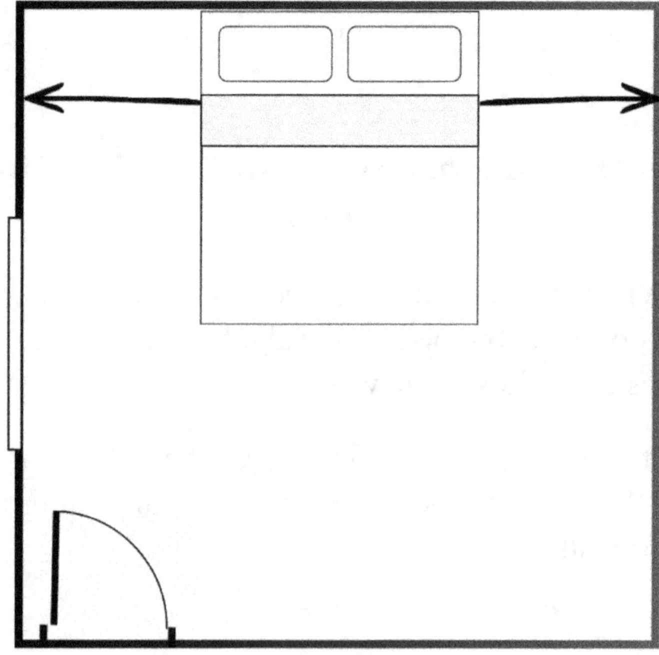

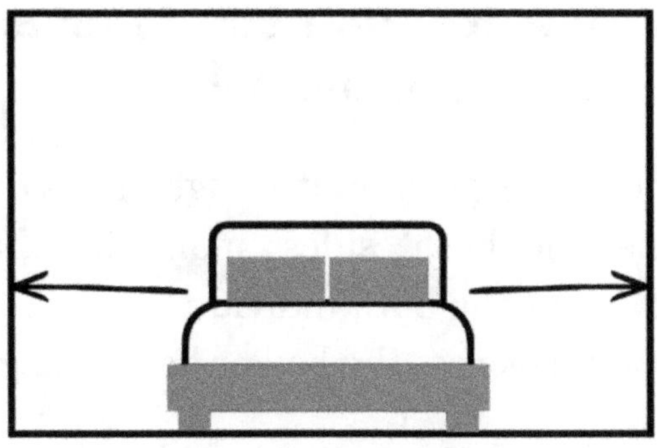

**Center bed on blank
wall**

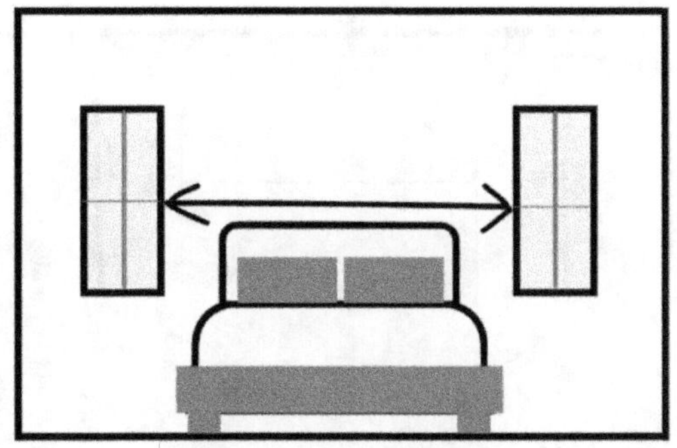

**Center bed between
two windows**

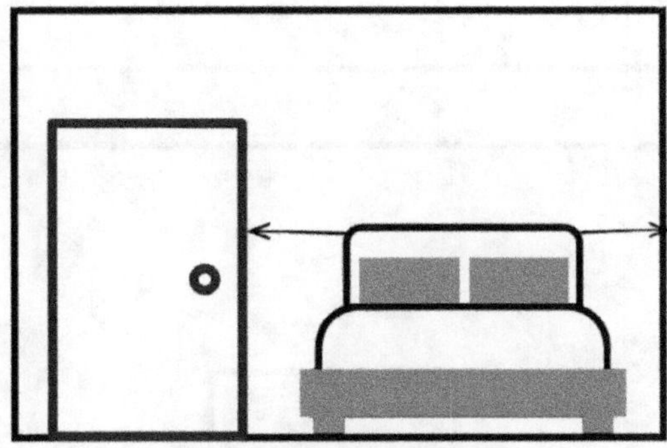

**Center bed between
door and wall**

Step Three: Place Nightstands on Both Sides of the Bed

Once the bed is in place, put a nightstand on each side. Having one on both sides maintains balance and accessibility, allowing both individuals to set things down without reaching across the bed or having to get up.

Nightstands should be similar in size, height, and shape even if they aren't identical. If you don't have a lot of space, use micro tables or hang shelves on either side.

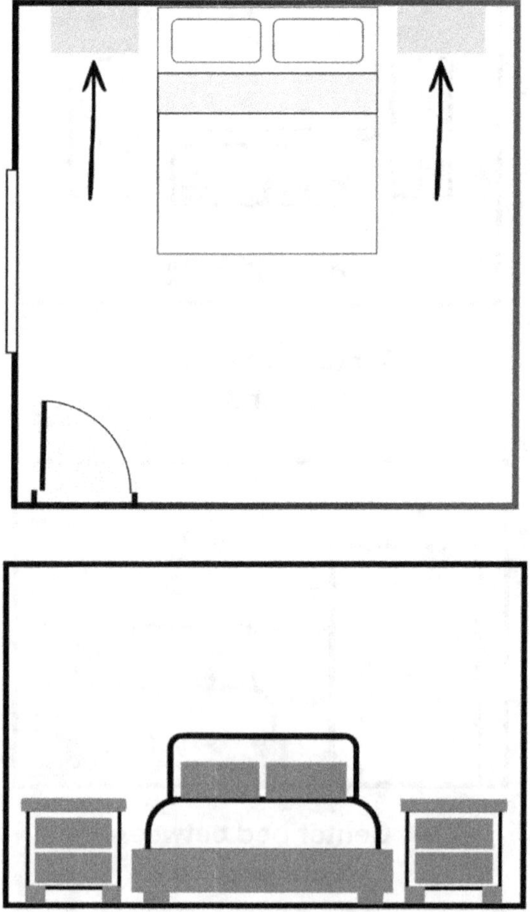

Step Four: Add Lighting Where It Is Used

Place a lamp on each nightstand or mount rechargeable light fixtures on the wall on either side. This allows you to turn the light on or off without getting out of bed.

Choose a lamp or light fixture that complements the size of the nightstands. If the lamp feels too big or too small, switch to a more suitable size to ensure a balanced look.

Step Five: Large Artwork Over the Bed

Position one large piece of artwork or a collage centered above the bed. Ensure that the artwork or collage stretches nearly as wide as the bed.

Hang the artwork low enough so that it sits a few inches above the headboard, creating a connection with the bed. If it's hung too high, it will feel too far from the bed. If it's too low, it may feel crowded. Adjust the height until it achieves a balanced appearance.

**One large piece of
artwork**

**Multiple pieces of
artwork**

If you don't have a headboard, hang the artwork high enough so you can sit up in bed without leaning against it. When making the bed, stand the pillows up on the ends to create the illusion of a headboard.

Step Six: Use a Rug to Define the Sleeping Area

Place an area rug under the bed so your feet touch it when you get out of bed. The rug should extend on both sides of the bed and past the foot to be functional. If the rug is too small, it'll look out of place.

For full to king-size beds, I recommend using a rug that is at least 8'x10'.

The rug helps define the sleeping area, even in small rooms, preventing the bed from feeling like it's floating. It contributes to a more organized and complete look in the space.

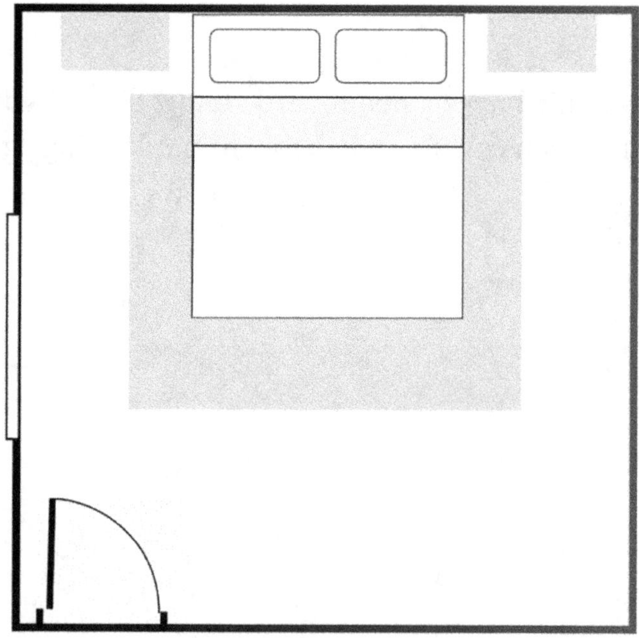

Large Rug: Good Size

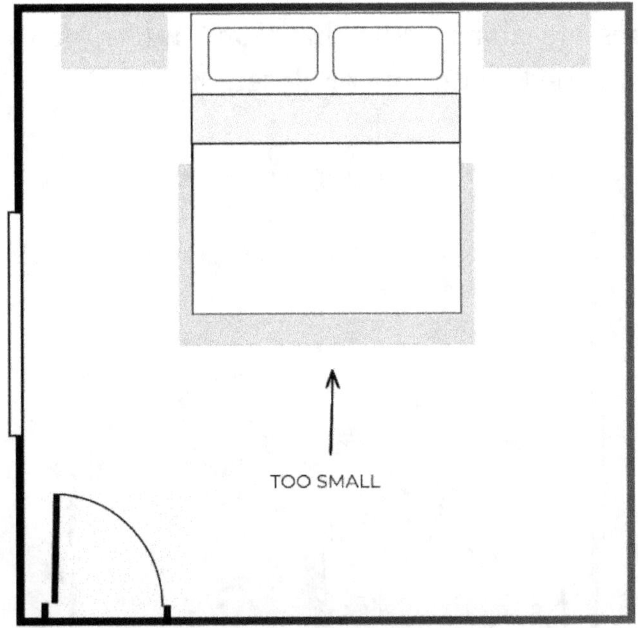

Small Rug: Too Small

Step Seven: Place Dresser

Place dressers along walls that don't interrupt walking paths to the bed, bathroom or closet.

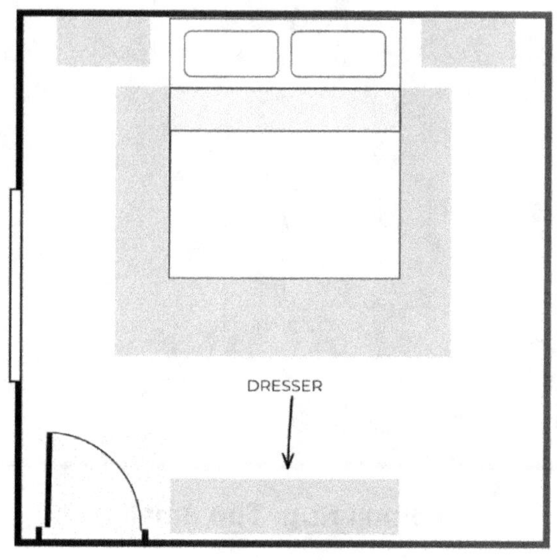

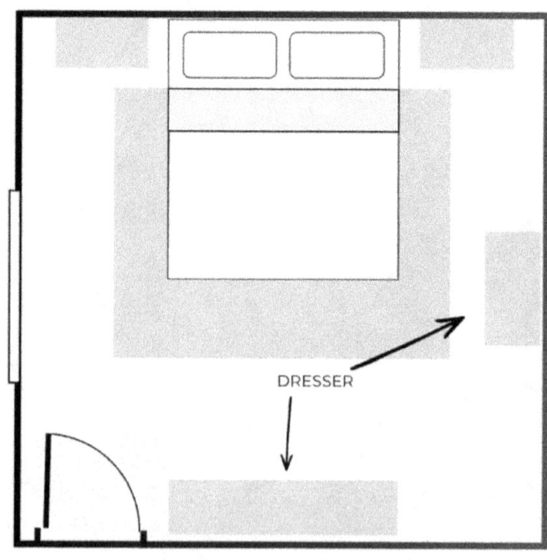

Step Eight: Hanging Curtains

Hang curtains as high and wide as possible to make windows appear larger. This creates a luxurious and grand look in the room.

The windows in the picture are the exact same size, but look at the difference that correct sized curtains make.

Correct　　　　　　　　　　**Too Short**

For 8' ceilings hang 90-96" curtains.

For 9' ceilings hang 102-108" curtains.

For 10' ceilings hang 120" curtains.

Hide charging cords

Charging cords shouldn't block walking paths.

If there's only one outlet behind the bed, use two extension cords or power strips. Plug both into the outlet and run each strip to either side of the bed. This will allow you to connect a lamp and a charging cord on both sides.

Remove Anything That Does Not Support Rest

You removed a lot in the Space Edit Reset, but as you arrange the bedroom, assess what no longer works in the space. If an item doesn't contribute to sleeping, dressing, or easy movement, consider removing it. Remove anything that complicates the room's functionality, rather than trying to make it fit.

How You Know the Bedroom Is Arranged Correctly

The bed is the focal point of the room, with nightstands on either side to create symmetry.

Paths around the bed, as well as to and from the bathroom and closet, are clear and accessible. The room maintains its organization daily, requiring no fixing. A well-arranged bedroom promotes easy rest.

Arranging the Living Room

Arranging a living room begins by observing what features it naturally highlights. Each living room has a focal point that draws attention, such as a fireplace, TV, large window, or built-in shelves. When the space feels off, it often results from furniture not being arranged around that main focal point.

After completing the Space Edit Reset, the living room's focal point becomes more apparent.

With unnecessary items removed and walkways cleared, your eyes will naturally be drawn to the same spot as you enter the room.

As you survey the room, take note of how it feels.

Step One: Identify the Focal Point

Stand at the main entrance to the living room and observe where your eyes are drawn first. The focal point is the area your eyes naturally return to. The layout of the room will be centered around this focal point. If there isn't a distinct focal point, you'll create one. If the room has a TV, it will likely serve as the focal point.

You can have a fireplace and a TV on separate walls, while still making the TV wall the primary focal point. The TV doesn't have to be mounted over the fireplace. If the room's layout allows for combining both features, that can work well, too.

I once had a client whose TV was mounted over the fireplace in the main living room. This setup caused the furniture to be crammed at one end of the long room, resulting in the family completely avoiding the space.

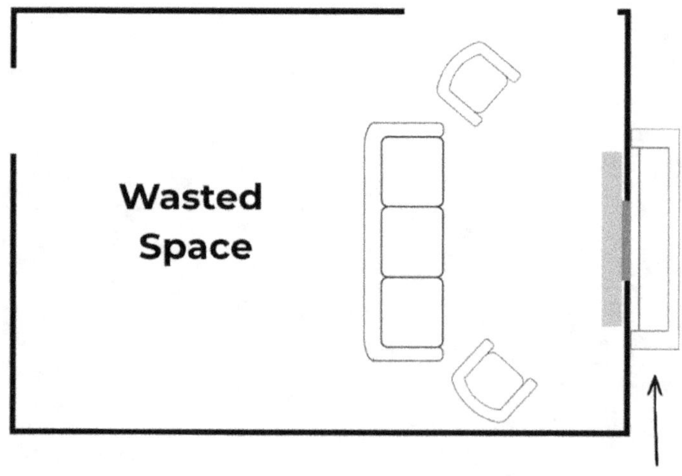

I unmounted the TV from over the fireplace, and placed a large piece of artwork in its place. I turned the whole layout of the room and mounted the TV on a wall perpendicular to the fireplace. Then I arranged all the furniture so the TV was now the main focal point in the room.

This allowed for a larger seating area with room for more seating. It's now a welcoming space and the family automatically gravitates toward this space on a daily basis and it's the perfect hosting spot for large gatherings.

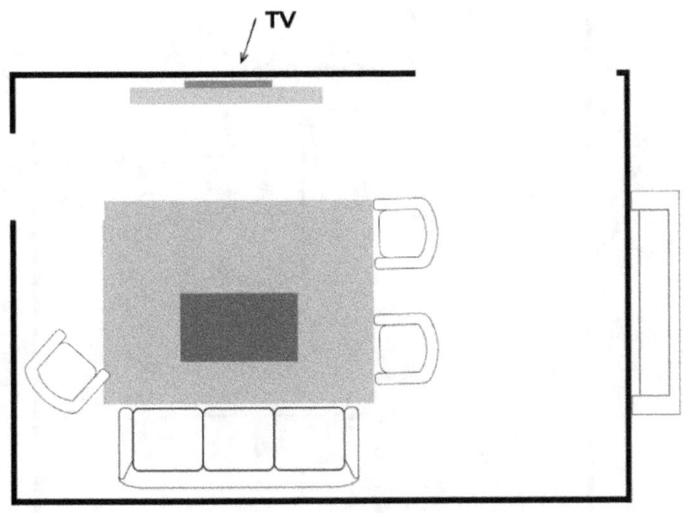

Step Two: Place the Main Seating in Relation to the Focal Point

Once you find the focal point, set the main seating to face it. The sofa should point straight toward the focal point.

After placing the sofa, sit down and look toward the focal point. It should feel easy and natural to see it.

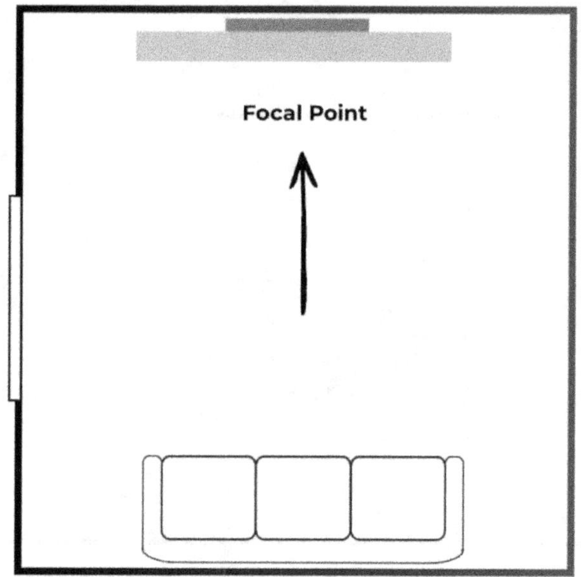

Step Three: Use a Rug to Hold the Seating Area Together

Place an area rug under the seating area to keep the furniture grouped together.

Choose an appropriately sized rug. Aim for a minimum rug size of 8'x10'. A 5'x7' rug is generally too small and can make a living space look disjointed and unfinished. A rug that fits well helps the seating area feel clear and organized.

Position the front legs of the sofa and chairs on the rug. This visual anchor defines the conversation area and gives the room a clean and organized feel.

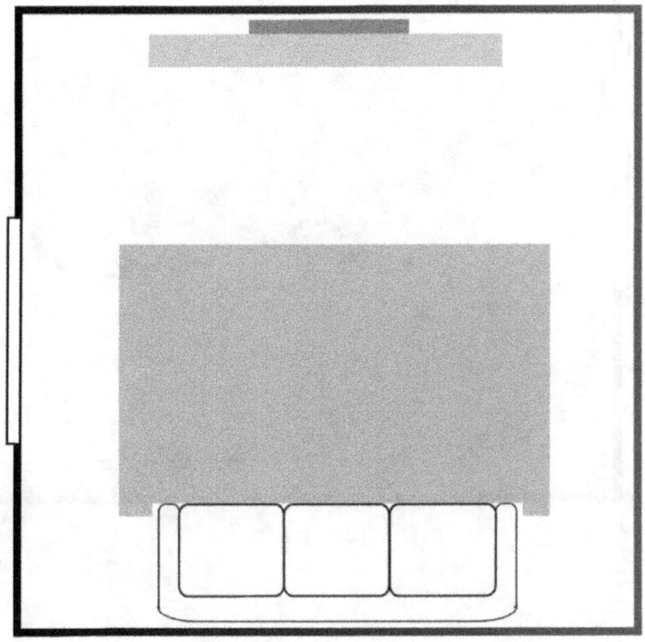

Step Four: Establish the Center Surface

After arranging the seating, place a coffee table in the middle of the group.

The coffee table should be close enough that everyone on the sofa can reach without standing or stretching too far.

Make sure the size of the table is appropriate. Not too big or too small.

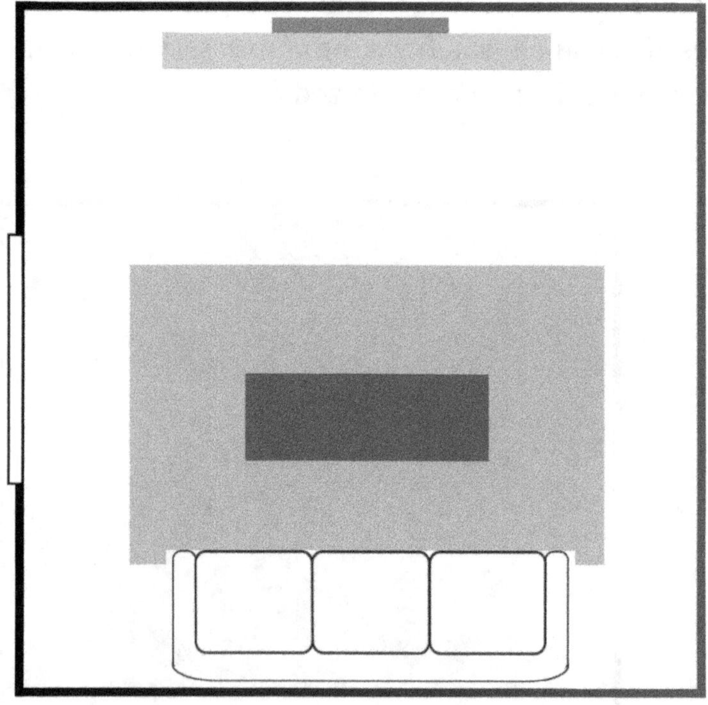

Step Five: Add Secondary Seating to Support Conversation

After the sofa and rug is in place, add chairs to complete the seating area and make it easy to talk with others.

Place the chairs so they feel like part of the same group as the sofa. They should face toward the center of the room and toward the main feature of the space.

Sit in each seat to check the spacing. If it feels awkward or too far apart, move the chairs closer or change their angle until it feels easy to use.

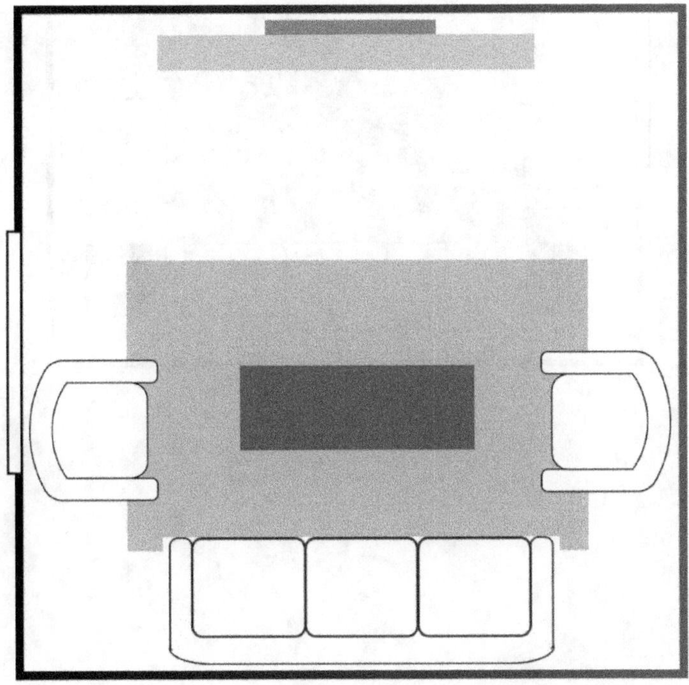

Step Six: End Tables

If space allows, position end tables on the ends of sofas or in between individual chairs. In tighter spaces, opt for micro tables to still provide a surface for drinks.

Ensure that end tables don't block pathways into seating areas, allowing for easy movement and access.

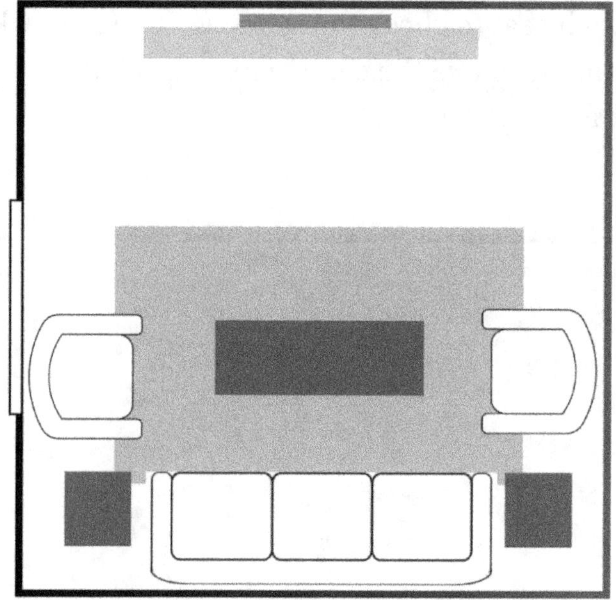

Step Seven: Remove What Competes with the Focal Point or Movement

As the room comes together, identify anything that obstructs movement or distracts from the main feature of the room.

This could be extra chairs blocking walkways, small tables placed in high traffic areas, or furniture pushed against walls with no clear purpose. If an item forces people to step around it or draws attention away from the center of the room, it should be relocated.

Move these items to a more appropriate room or evaluate whether they still belong in your home. The living room should facilitate easy movement and be easier to use, not harder.

How You Know the Living Room Is Arranged Correctly

You'll know the living room is set up effectively when it functions smoothly without any conscious effort.

- Guests know where to sit upon entering.
- Conversations flow easily without needing to rearrange chairs.
- Pathways remain clear for easy movement, even when the space is occupied.
- Furniture stays in its designated place and no one feels the need to pull seating closer or push tables aside.

Arranging the Dining Room

Arranging a dining room begins with understanding how people will navigate through the space. The room functions best when individuals can easily walk in, pull out a chair, sit down, stand up, and move around the table without bumping into things.

When a dining room feels uncomfortable or is seldomly used, it's often because the table or chairs are blocking easy movement.

After completing the Space Edit Reset™, the dining room should be clear of unnecessary furniture and items that obstruct movement. What remains should be placed to promote easy gathering and movement. The goal is to create a simple-to-use room.

The table is the focal point in the room. Its placement determines whether the dining room feels easy to use or requires constant adjustments.

Step One: Place the Table

The table should be positioned according to the room's layout first, rather than aligning it with the light fixture.

Many homes have ceiling lights that were installed off-center. Avoid adjusting the table to match the light, as this can create awkward flow and make the room appear uneven.

Center the table within the usable dining area to ensure walking paths are logical and the space feels balanced. Once the table is properly positioned, if the light fixture resembles a chandelier, the light should be centered directly over the table.

Use a simple ceiling hook to swing the light position over so it falls directly over the center of the table. This allows the table to remain in its proper place while aligning the light properly.

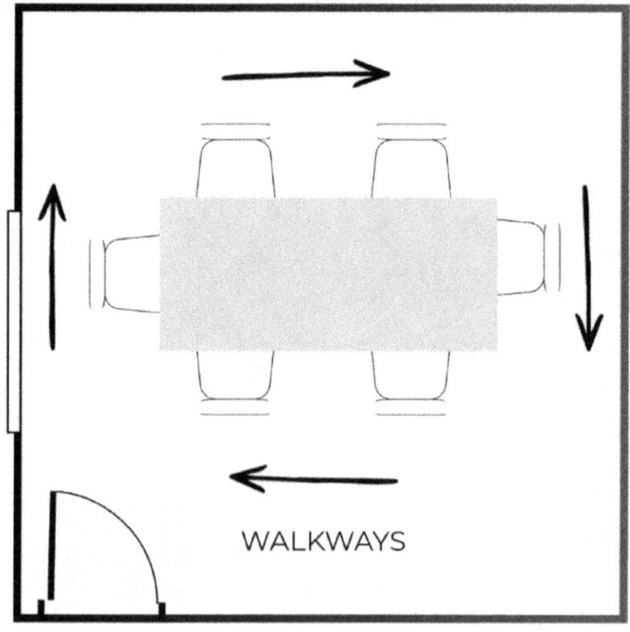

Step Two: Place the Rug (If Used)

Once the table is positioned, decide whether you want to place a rug underneath it.

The rug should be large enough to accommodate all the chairs, even when they are pulled out. If chairs catch on the edge or roll off the rug, it indicates that the rug is too small and may create obstacles.

Check each chair to ensure it remains on the rug when someone sits down or stands up. If the rug can't accommodate this, remove it or upgrade to a larger one.

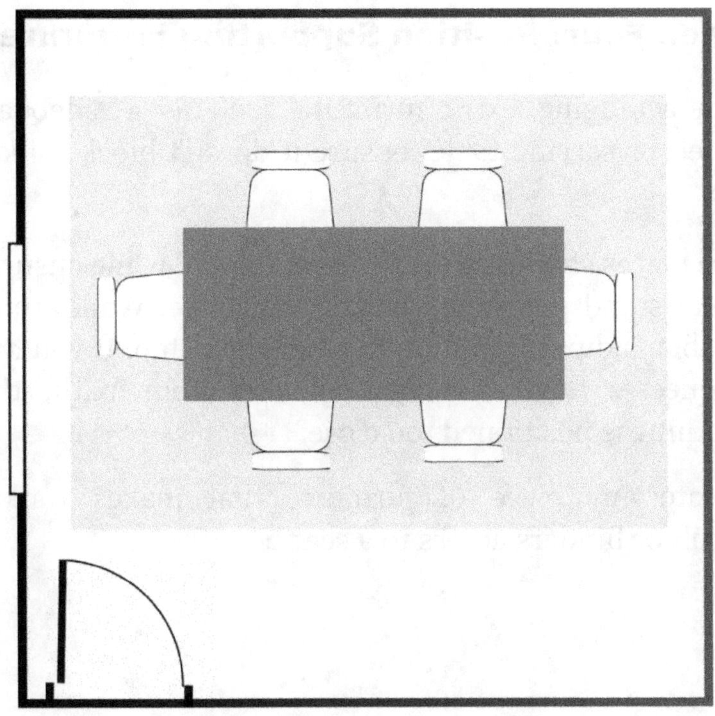

Step Three: Position the Chairs

Once the table is positioned, place chairs on each side. Ensure that someone can sit down and stand up without bumping into a wall, cabinet, or other furniture. Then, walk behind each pulled-out chair to confirm that you can pass through easily.

Space the chairs evenly around the table. Each chair should have enough space to slide in and out without bumping into the one next to it. The goal is to ensure there's enough space for people to sit comfortably and for others to move around them effortlessly.

Step Four: Position Supporting Furniture

When arranging extra furniture such as a sideboard, cabinet, or serving table, ensure it doesn't block walking paths.

These pieces should store dishes and food, while ensuring all chairs and pathways remain accessible. Walk around the table and pay attention to where you step. If you have to squeeze, turn sideways, or alter your path, then something is positioned too close.

Relocate any piece of furniture that makes walking difficult or hinders access to a seat.

When the Dining Room Is Arranged Correctly

You'll know the dining room is set up well when:

- People can sit down and stand up without moving furniture around.
- Chairs slide in and out easily.
- Walking paths remain open even when everyone is seated.
- All seats feel easy to use.
- No area feels tight or blocked.

A well-designed dining room makes movement easy, so sitting down for meals feels comfortable. When the table is positioned correctly and there's enough space to walk around it, the room functions effectively without needing any adjustments.

Arranging the Office

Arranging an office starts with how you walk into the room and what happens when you sit down to work.

A well-designed office should enhance your work, allowing you to work without constantly rearranging your environment. When an office setup fails, you might think you just can't concentrate, but the real issue is how the room is configured.

Once the Space Edit Reset™ is complete, the office should already be clear of items that don't contribute to productivity. Desks and surfaces should be clear and accessible, allowing for easy visibility and use. Walking in and out of the room should feel simple and open. Remaining items should be arranged to facilitate immediate work, enabling you to maintain focus without interruptions.

The desk is the central piece in the office, and its placement influences your ability to focus. All other furniture should be arranged around the desk to create a supportive workspace.

Step One: Place the Desk

Begin by determining which direction you should face while working.

There are two desk setups that can enhance your workspace when done intentionally. Either one is fine. The key is to select one and place the desk fully in that position. Leaving it halfway often leads to constant moving and fixing.

Option One: Desk Against a Wall With Your Back to the Center of the Room

Position the desk against a wall so you face the wall, and your back is to the center of the room while sitting.

Do you feel comfortable with your back to the door or the center of the room?

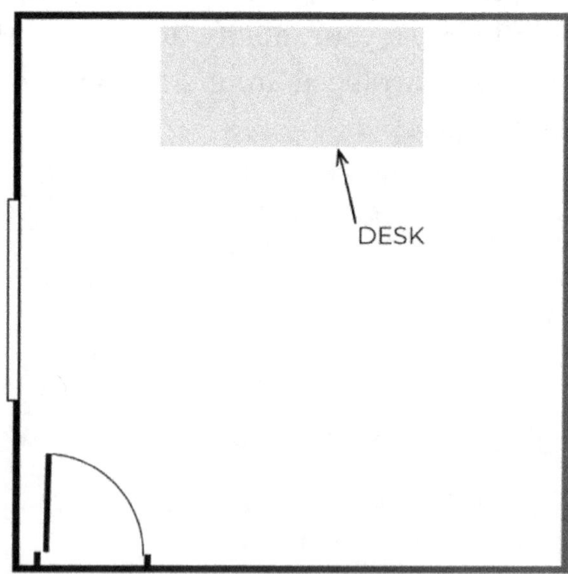

Option Two: Desk Facing the Room with Your Back to a Wall

If you prefer to face the center of the room while working, position the desk so that a wall is behind you. This setup is ideal for video calls, as the wall provides a clean background or a great place to hang large artwork.

Position the desk far enough away from the wall so you can sit down, stand up, and walk away easily.

If the desk is too close to the wall behind you, the space may feel tight, causing you to constantly shift your chair or desk.

Once the desk is in place, walk into the room, sit down, stand up, and leave as you normally would. It should feel smooth and simple. If you have to squeeze around furniture, move the desk until walking feels easy.

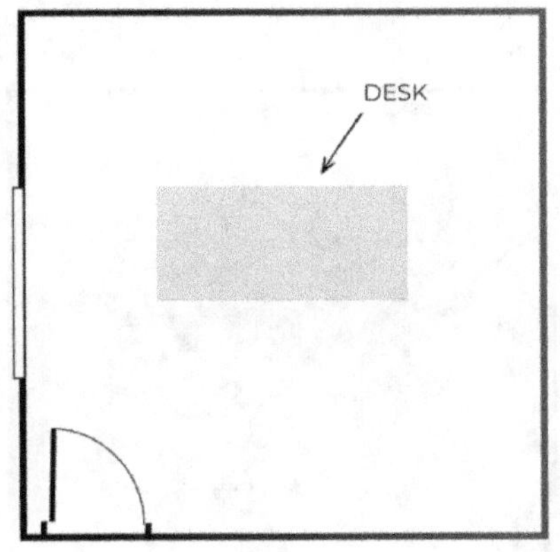

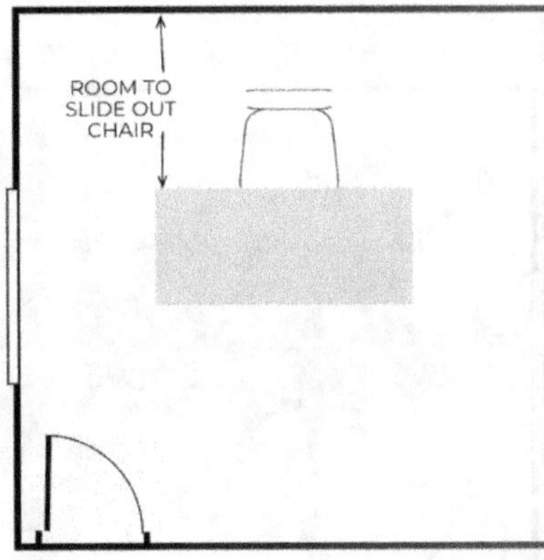

Step Two: Place Storage to Support Focus

Next, position storage to enhance your workflow.

Things you use every day should be within reach while sitting at your desk. Items you occasionally use should be accessible without having to shift major items in the room.

It's most effective when your essential items are beside you or in front of you.

If you find yourself walking across the room several times a day to retrieve something, move it closer to improve efficiency.

If you have bookshelves, consider placing them in one of the following locations.

1. On either side of the desk.
2. Behind the desk, for an executive feel.
3. On an adjacent or opposite wall.

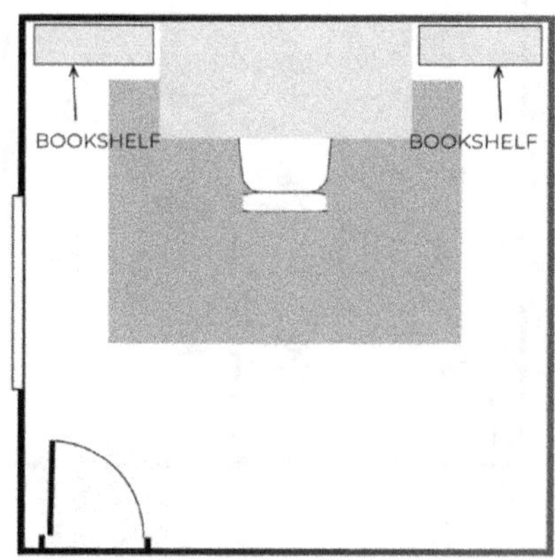

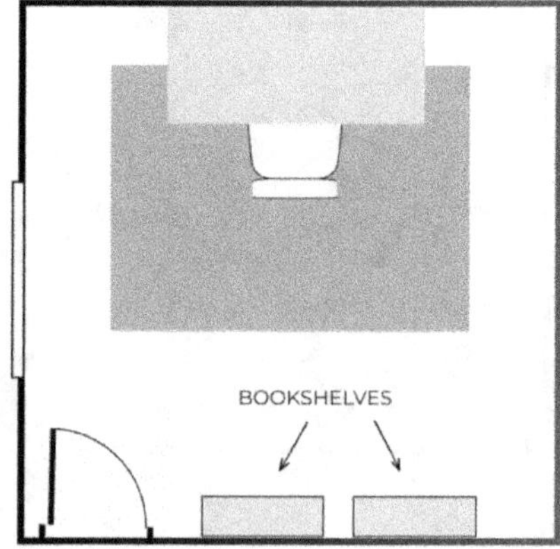

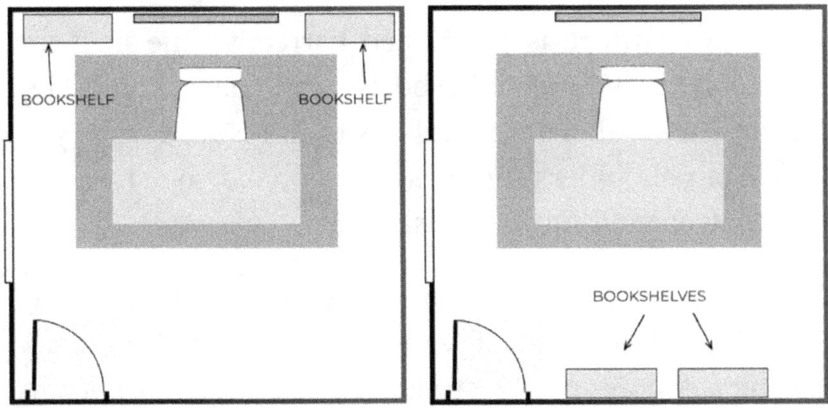

A cabinet for printers and supplies can be placed adjacent to or behind the desk.

Consider the proper placement of your storage furniture by sitting in your chair and swiveling. Are items like printers, pens, and frequently used files or books within arm's reach while you remain seated?

Step Three: Align the Work Setup

Once the furniture is positioned correctly, line up your work tools. Your screen, keyboard, and chair should face straight ahead, allowing your body to sit forward while you work. Your shoulders should stay even, and you shouldn't need to keep shifting your position.

Sit at the desk for a few minutes and notice how your body feels. If you find yourself leaning to one side, frequently shifting positions, or adjusting your seat often, it indicates that something needs to be moved. Change the setup until sitting feels easy and comfortable.

The desk should be proportionate to your body, allowing for a natural and steady working experience.

Step Four: Resolve Lighting

Good lighting should make work easier and more comfortable. The light shouldn't shine in your eyes or reflect off your screen. Ideally, you should be able to sit at your desk and work without constantly adjusting lamps or switching lights.

How to test it:

1. Sit at your desk and notice how the light feels.

2. If you see glare, dark shadows, or find yourself repeatedly repositioning the lamp, adjust the light source until it's even and pleasant.

Step Five: Address the Floor and Chair Movement

If there's a rug in the office, place it so your chair can glide smoothly across the floor.

Your chair should roll or glide freely without catching on the rug's edges. If the rug catches the wheels or makes movement harder, it will distract you while you work.

If the chair feels rough or hard to move, shift the rug or take it out so the floor stays smooth and easy to use.

Step Six: Observe Use and Remove Interference

Observe and remove distractions while you work. Notice chairs that collect books, desks that become cluttered, or furniture that gets in the way when you stand. These issues become apparent during everyday use, so address them as soon as you spot them.

When the Office Is Arranged Correctly

You'll know the office is set up well when:

- You can walk in, sit down, and start working right away without moving anything.
- You stay seated longer without shifting around. Standing up and walking away from the desk feels easy.
- You're done working, you can leave the room without needing to clean up first.

Arranging a Teen's Bedroom

Arranging a teen's bedroom begins with recognizing that the room has to support many activities. Teens sleep, study, relax, and spend time with friends there. When the room isn't organized to support these needs clearly, teens end up using the bed, floor, and every surface for everything, which leads to clutter and frustration.

After the Space Edit Reset is complete, the room should already be clear of items from younger years. Furniture should fit the teen's size and daily routines. Surfaces should be clear and easy to use. Walking through the room should feel simple and open. Everything that remains should be positioned so the space supports studying, relaxing, and sleeping without constant rearranging.

The bed remains the focal point in the room, but the space should also include areas for homework and hanging out, so everything doesn't happen on the bed.

Step One: Place the Bed as the Fixed Anchor

Start by placing the head of the bed against a wall where it feels steady and doesn't block walking space. The bed doesn't have to be centered on the wall, but it should allow for easy access to make the bed each morning.

Aim for symmetry where possible, but prioritize flexible, multi-use layouts.

Ensure your teen can get in and out of bed easily and move around the room without bumping into furniture. If the bed feels crowded or obstructs traffic, relocate it before arranging any other pieces.

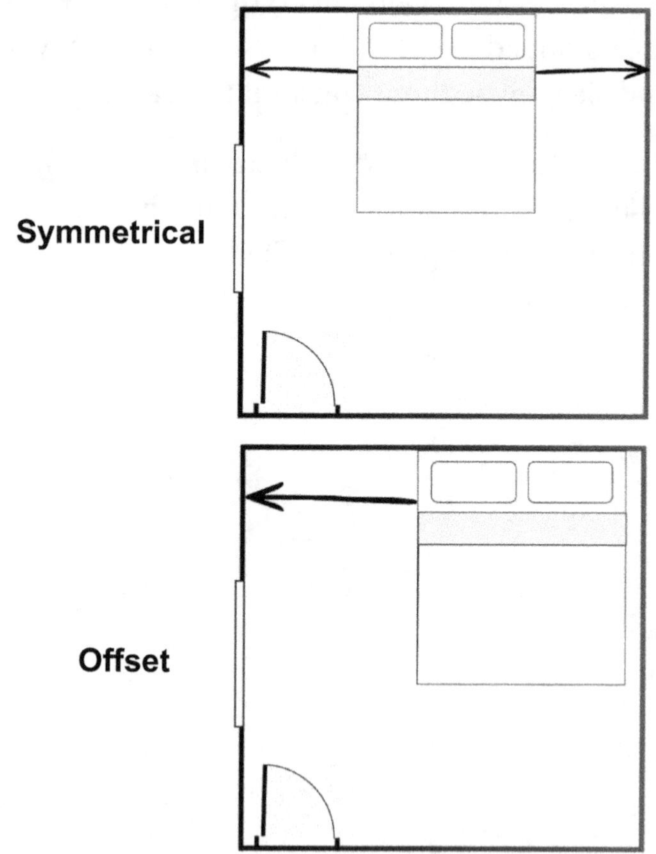

Step Two: Add a Small Surface Near the Bed

After the bed is positioned, add a nightstand (shelf, desk, or small wall ledge) within easy reach.

Keep only the items your teen uses at night and in the morning, like a lamp, phone charger, book, or water bottle on that surface. When too many things pile up, the area gets messy and harder to use. The goal is to keep essentials within arm's reach while minimizing clutter.

Step Three: Establish a Clear Study Zone

If possible, set up a separate work area with a desk, chair, and lighting to keep homework away from the bed. This keeps the sleeping area distinct from the studying zone, reducing distractions.

This area should let them sit down and begin working without having to move blankets, pillows, or furniture first.

Place the desk where the chair can slide in and out easily. Make sure the light is bright enough for reading or screen time without shining in their eyes.

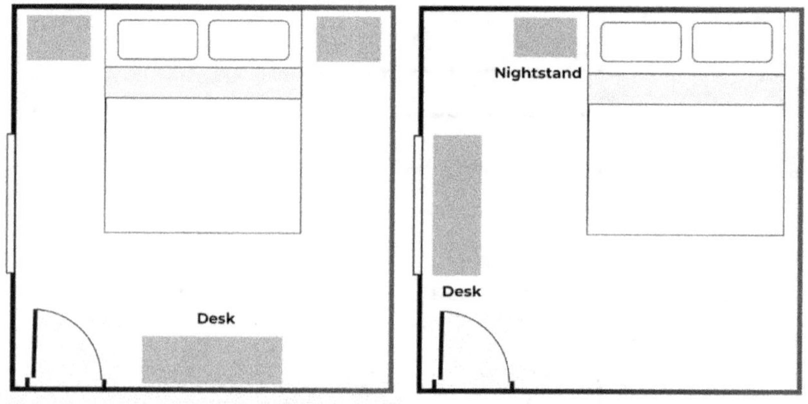

Keep school supplies within arm's reach so your teen doesn't have to walk across the room to grab studying essentials. When homework ends up on the bed, work often gets put off. A clear work area helps your teen focus and keep a routine.

Step Four: Create a Social Use Area

Teens use their rooms to spend time with friends, both in person and online. Therefore, the space should include a place for sitting, talking, and relaxing that isn't the bed. When everything happens on the bed, it becomes harder to rest, harder to study, and harder to keep the room organized.

If space allows, set up a small hangout area, such as open floor space with pillows, a chair in the corner, a bean bag, or a small couch to give your teen a place to sit and connect with friends.

Place the hang-out area away from both the bed, and the desk if possible. Keeping sleeping, studying, and relaxing in separate areas makes the room feel clearer, and helps daily routines run more smoothly.

With a dedicated spot for social time, teens are less likely to scatter their belongings across every surface. The space stays cleaner, feels calmer, and better supports how it's used each day.

Step Five: Place Clothing Storage Where It's Used

Clothing storage should support how the teen actually gets dressed.

When storage fights habit, clothing ends up on the floor or furniture. Placement should reduce effort rather than rely on discipline.

Step Six: Support Expression Without Overcrowding

A teen's room is filled with posters, artwork, collections, and personal items that reflect their interests and personality. Give these items a clear place instead of letting them scatter across the room.

Designate one wall, bookshelf, hanging shelf, bulletin board, or display area where your teen can hang or place their favorite things. This gives them space to express themselves while keeping the rest of the room easy to use and keep clean.

When personal belongings are kept in one main area, the room feels more organized and less crowded. This helps the space support both self-expression and everyday activities.

Step Seven: Observe Use and Adjust the Room

As your teen uses the room, pay attention to what keeps causing problems.

Identify surfaces that become clutter hotspots, furniture that blocks foot traffic, or storage that takes too many steps to use. These problems show up in how the room is used each day.

When an issue appears, change the room instead of blaming habits. A room that fits daily routines stays easier to use, creates fewer arguments, and keeps its setup longer.

When a Teen's Bedroom Is Arranged Correctly

You'll know a teen's bedroom is set up well when:

- It supports homework, hanging out, and rest without needing constant fixing.
- The bed is used for sleeping only.
- The desk is used for schoolwork.
- The room adjusts easily as daily routines change.

A well-designed bedroom setup helps teens move through this stage of life more smoothly. The room should support their growing responsibilities and activities and make everyday life easier.

AFTER THE RESET

After the Space Edit Reset, your room begins working quietly in the background of your life. You walk in and use it immediately. You sit down without moving anything first. You set things on clear surfaces where they belong. You leave without fixing or shifting a single thing.

The space holds together in everyday life, so your focus stays on what you're doing rather than on the room.

The room now has a clear purpose and an easy flow. Walking paths stay open. Furniture supports how you move and rest. Surfaces stay usable, because everything has a place, small shifts are easy to notice and quick to fix.

When something feels off, you move one item, clear one spot, or open a path, and the room returns to working smoothly.

You begin to trust your space. Tasks feel lighter because the room no longer adds extra steps. You don't watch it, manage it, or constantly adjust it.

The room does its job without pulling energy from you. You move through your day with less friction. Simple things feel simple again.

Life keeps changing, and the room keeps supporting you through it. Short projects live in one area and then leave.

Guests can come and go without throwing the space off. Work can move into the home for a season and stay organized. The room stretches when needed and settles back into place with ease.

Sometimes a room truly needs a new purpose. A bedroom becomes shared. An office becomes a guest room. A child's space grows with them. When these moments arrive, you can see them clearly and reset the room with confidence. The process feels familiar and steady. You set a new starting point and move forward without second-guessing yourself.

This steadiness changes how your nervous system feels in your home every day. You pause before adding more things. You use what you already have. The space stays solid instead of shifting with every busy week or tired day. It supports your routines, your rest, your work, and your growth.

Rooms stop feeling like projects you have to keep working on. Cleaning feels lighter. Adjusting furniture stops being part of your routine. The time and energy that once went into constant fixing now stays with your life.

Your home becomes a place you rely on. Not because it looks perfect, but because it works. It holds its shape. It supports your movement. It makes daily tasks easier instead of harder.

The Space Edit Reset is about having a space that supports who you are right now and can adjust as you grow.

Life continues to move forward.
Your room continues to work.

Your nervous system feels calm and welcome in your space. Now you can love your home and focus more on the people and activities in your life.

Welcome Home.

What's next...

THE TRANSFORMATIVE HOME EXPERIENCE

Now that your rooms are properly arranged and have been reset, you can elevate your home to the next level through color, style and décor. Book the Transformative Home Experience.

We'll meet virtually through Zoom and discuss an elevated vision for your space. You'll receive a clear plan with more detailed room arrangements, color choices, furniture, accessories, and drapery selections.

You'll receive shoppable links for every new selection we create, along with a clear plan of execution.

Your room will not only function perfectly, but you'll fall in love with every color, texture, pattern, and textile that truly reflects your personal style.

Book your **Transformative Home Experience.**

As part of the Transformative Home Experience, if you haven't already, you'll need to finish the 6 steps of the Space Edit Reset before we meet on Zoom. However, you won't be required to go through the arranging process, as we'll cover that in detail in our Zoom session and in the new room plan, I provide you.

What's included with the Transformative Home Experience:

- The Space Edit Reset™ online video course (If you've already purchased the online course version, you'll receive a discount towards the purchase of the Transformative Home Experience.)
- One 90-minute virtual video call planning session.
- 30 days of unlimited access to me through messages and videos on Voxxer for any questions and assistance you need.
- A floorplan of your new room layout.
- Color palette.
- A list of executable tasks to complete the look of your room.
- A list of shoppable links to all product recommendations.

To book your Transformative Home Experience, go to

www.vividxhouse.com/transformative-home-experience

Once you've completed this book and done the Space Edit Reset steps in your own home, tell 3 other people about the reset who you think this would transform their homes and lives.

<u>Share your before and after photos online!</u>

Use #SpaceEditReset

Tag: @TheVividXHouse

Facebook Group:
Space Edit Reset

Instagram:
@TheVividXHouse

TikTok:
@TheVividXHouse